THE
EMPOWERMENT
PARADIGM

THE
EMPOWERMENT
PARADIGM

A Transformative, People Oriented Management
Strategy With A Proven Track Record

A. M. NOBEL

To order additional copies of this book, contact:
Xlibris Corporation
1-888-795-4274
www.Xlibris.com
Orders@Xlibris.com
96775

CONTENTS

Introduction

L et's get one thing straight from the start. This is not a newfangled business theory or a hypothesis based upon logical conjecture, neither is it a condescending treatise, strewn with management-speak, which says much but means little.

> CAN BE UNIVERSALLY APPLIED TO ORGANIZATIONS OF ALL TYPES AND ALL SECTORS

I have spent years thinking about how best to put what is essentially a distillation of my career as a senior executive into a format that not only properly expresses the fulfillment and joy I have experienced in helping individuals and organizations realize their potential, but can also be universally applied to organizations of all types and all sectors so as to reach the widest possible audience.

I have read various tomes on business methodologies, which chronicle the experiences of other senior executives, but these nearly always seem an exercise in vanity and egocentrism. I don't want to regale the reader with a tale of how I did this or that. Instead, I want to help explain how to make *your* organization a success by mobilizing your employees and harnessing their contributions and ideas in order to strengthen your organization while allowing these employees to share the fruits of their collective labor.

So what is the Empowerment Paradigm?

Put simply, the Empowerment Paradigm is a methodology that focuses upon realizing the potential of each of the most fundamental units within an organization—the individual employee.

A STEADFAST REGARD TO THE FREEDOM OF THE INDIVIDUAL EMPLOYEE

And it works. The Empowerment Paradigm is the culmination of decades of experience in executive management in multinational organizations. Employed in several different organizations since the late 1960s, the philosophy espoused within the Empowerment Paradigm has worked on each occasion. Its latest incarnation has been fully tested by the 2008-2009 global recession: while all but the most ill-conceived and poorly administered companies can achieve at least a modicum of success in a growing economy, it speaks volumes when an organization thrives and increases its market share during a severe economic downturn.

The methodology employs a multistranded approach, which has, as a focus, a steadfast regard to the freedom of the individual employee, enabling all employees to maximize their potential and increase their personal fulfillment and reward. It is through the unique methodology of the Empowerment Paradigm that other organizational improvements fall naturally into place and become entrenched in the long run.

Empowering employees and making them stakeholders in an organization is not, I realize, in and of itself, a new concept nor is the congruence of socialist egalitarianism and capitalist incentives espoused by the philosophy. However, the Empowerment Paradigm brings a multifaceted approach to the concept, explaining how success can be achieved and what benefits ensue in a practical way that can be adopted by all organizations.

After the strands of the methodology have been carefully implemented, as described in the early chapters of the book, the Empowerment Paradigm ethos automatically facilitates a series of organizational improvements. This is the unique aspect of this business philosophy—the Empowerment Paradigm Difference. These improvements, examined in the latter part of the book, are driven by employees, who have been given the freedom and confidence to satisfy their expectations, who have a greater say in determining their own future, and who create room for their own reward by increasing shareholder value and benefiting from a proportion of this. In essence, the Empowerment Paradigm creates a prism through which the organizational improvement can be realized.

This book is primarily designed as a guide for ambitious and committed organizational leaders who are seeking to improve the fortunes of an organization.

If you are the kind of leader who dictates, delegates, and sits back to deal with the consequences, read no further. If, on the other hand, you are the kind of leader who is prepared to lead by example, from the front, to become directly involved in tackling problems, to nurture the talents of employees, and to personally ensure that success is rewarded, read on.

There are four fundamental strands that underpin the Empowerment Paradigm:

THE REMOVAL OF FEAR

The fundamental precept of the Empowerment Paradigm and the key to releasing the talents and aspirations of employees

THE BUILDING OF A POSITIVE, FLEXIBLE, EAGER-TO-SELF-IMPROVE TEAM

Empowering employees allows an organization to build a team whose goal is to improve its own performance

THE ESTABLISHMENT OF OPERATIONAL AND ETHICAL IDENTITY (VISION, MISSION, AND VALUES)

Essential to ensuring an organization has a firm direction of travel and a moral compass

The ultimate objective of the Empowerment Paradigm is to allow employees the freedom and confidence to work autonomously without the fear and the constraint of prohibitive corporate monitoring—in other words, to lighten bureaucratic oversight.

> ALLOW EMPLOYEES THE FREEDOM AND CONFIDENCE TO WORK AUTONOMOUSLY WITHOUT FEAR.

Deregulation is not a popular concept in the post-credit crunch economy, but this is to conflate the promotion of operational efficiency with recklessness. The Empowerment Paradigm employs sufficient checks and balances to satisfy the requirements of risk management without imposing unnecessary restraint upon individual and collective innovations and aspirations, which drive diversification and growth.

The Empowerment Paradigm sets out a clear, step-by-step approach to meeting the ultimate objective.

The starting point is an organization that is floundering in a sea of fear and lack of confidence borne of stringent operational controls. A pervading atmosphere of fear is a common condition in such organizations but may not fit your own circumstances exactly. This need not deter as the core methodology can be applied to the betterment of any organization.

The first chapter examines what employees want. Understanding this is the fundamental precept that underpins how the Empowerment Paradigm is implemented.

The second chapter explores the virtues of the first three fundamental strands of the strategy—the removal of fear; building a positive, flexible, eager-to-self-improve team; and improving collective and individual morale.

The third chapter considers the importance of establishing an apposite organizational and ethical identity, which identifies the minimum levels of honesty, integrity, and trust expected of all employees.

The fourth chapter examines the vital role of the organizational leader in driving through the methodology in a manner that is consistent with the organizational and ethical identity. It shows how—when an organizational leader acts with respect, honesty, compassion, and integrity—employees grow to trust that an organization has their best interests at heart and this, in turn, enhances confidence, stability, and hope for the future.

The fifth chapter addresses how the Empowerment Paradigm organization differs from other organizations through its transformation brought about by adopting these methodologies and how this translates into meaningful, self-sustained organizational improvements. These improvements have occurred naturally, without fail, whenever I have followed the principles espoused by the Empowerment Paradigm. Such areas of improvement include refocusing operational orientation, simplification of function and documentation, quality, health and safety, environmental, optimization, establishing organizational size, reducing costs, sales and proposals, and team building.

Applied through the parameters laid down by the Empowerment Paradigm, these organizational improvements will be shown to be less disruptive and significantly more effective than merely embarking upon a series of direct organizational improvements. Clear and detailed examples show how the Empowerment Paradigm facilitates these improvements and demonstrate that if the strictures of the Empowerment Paradigm are properly instituted, improvements and optimization will automatically flow in many key operational areas. This self-adjustment is what separates the Empowerment Paradigm from other business philosophies. This added value, the Empowerment Paradigm Difference, is shown to be the engine of organizational growth and prosperity. Case studies are included in the chapter to help illustrate the principles espoused. These are necessarily anonymous but are based on real-life business experiences that I have come across.

The sixth chapter describes the final structure and characteristics of the Empowerment Paradigm organization once the recommendations in the first four chapters have been properly implemented and the automatic improvements described in chapter 5 have been realized. In essence, this chapter shows the many ways in which all employees are empowered to exceed their previous expectations in their working life.

> THE PRINCIPLE OF EMPOWERING EMPLOYEES IS TRANSFORMATIVE.

I have spent decades refining this business methodology in real-life circumstances where the difference between success and failure is measured in terms of the livelihood of employees and the fortunes of shareholders. The principle of empowering those same employees to improve their individual circumstances via collective success is transformative, and the results have been wonderful to behold. I have also seen organizations, which I have left, disintegrate and improvements reversed in a remarkably short period once new leadership has turned its back upon the core methodology.

Empowering individuals to have a far greater say in determining their own future and level of reward and, in so doing, spectacularly improving an organization's commercial success is a process to which every progressive organizational leader should aspire. This book will help any such leader attain this laudable objective.

I trust that you will find it as useful in improving the performance of your organization as I have in transforming the fortunes of my own.

Chapter One

What Employees Want

What Employees Want

Before exploring the virtues of the first three strands of the Empowerment Paradigm methodology, it is vital to understand what employees want from their employment and working experience. By understanding what employees want, it is possible to develop a coherent and effective strategy to release them from unnecessary constraints and oppression and to set free their latent creativity and innovation. Without such an understanding, implementing the principles of the Empowerment Paradigm becomes an exercise in blind faith.

If employees are asked what they want, invariably, job security and job satisfaction are priorities.

THE DESIRE TO BE PART OF SOMETHING BIGGER THAN THEMSELVES

Job security is the natural product of a desire to provide for oneself and one's family. As explored later in this chapter, the Empowerment Paradigm does not only enhance the level of job security per se but ensures that it pervades the organizational culture and that the feeling of job security becomes ingrained within an employee's automatic expectation.

Job satisfaction is a more nebulous concept, which is not easily defined. Job security feeds into this, but ultimately, job satisfaction will be perceived differently by every employee. To a lesser or greater extent, job satisfaction might mean each, or a combination, of the following:

WORKING ENVIRONMENT

Working within an environment where confidence and aspiration replace anxiety and the fear of failure

OPPORTUNITY

Being given the opportunity to grow professionally, and gain promotion, by developing existing skills and attaining new ones

GIVING

Giving to or helping others within, and also outside, the organization

CUSTOMER SATISFACTION

Satisfying customers through exemplary performance

Above all else, the Empowerment Paradigm releases a latent desire and the ability to realize a more powerful and fundamentally fulfilling aspect of job satisfaction—that is, the desire to be part of something bigger than oneself. In the Empowerment Paradigm organization, time and again, employees will find themselves acting beyond their previous expectations and, in so doing, transform themselves, their prospects, and as a consequence, the organization.

Inherently, all of us yearn to be part of the pack—to belong to a group that has a collective goal from which the personal security and the basic necessities of life can be derived. In modernity, a commercial organization is the most common manifestation of the pack. Through application of the Empowerment Paradigm methodologies, this basic pack instinct can be harnessed and wielded as a powerful motivational and wealth-creating tool.

Most employees will never start their own businesses or attain great wealth through their employment. But given the freedom, confidence, and responsibility to innovate, employees can be melded into creative and highly productive teams. In this way, each employee is given the opportunity to become part of something bigger than themselves, to utilize their gifts/talents to the betterment of the organization, to experience pride in their contribution to the collective organizational success, to know that they have personally made a difference and that they count for something, and to understand the gratification of personal reward and recognition for their efforts. These desires on the part of employees can be grouped as follows:

ACCEPTANCE

To be accepted within an organization and to know that the organization values what one has to offer

USE OF TALENTS

Wanting and being allowed to use gifts/talents that can make a positive contribution to the organization

ADDING VALUE

Adding to the value of the organization

MAKING A DIFFERENCE

Wanting and being allowed to make a difference and to count for something

RECOGNITION AND REWARD

Being recognized and rewarded for exemplary service and performance

The Empowerment Paradigm shows how to give employees what they want and, in so doing, enrich the organizational culture and well-being and attain enhanced commercial success.

Chapter Two

Removing the Shackles of Fear

The Impediment of Fear

Fear is a corrosive and debilitating emotion. It is an instinctive and primal response to circumstances that threaten our well-being. Brought into the workplace, fear inhibits operational efficiency, stifles creativity, and generates a plethora of human resource issues.

AN INSTINCTIVE AND PRIMAL RESPONSE TO CIRCUMSTANCES THAT THREATEN OUR WELL-BEING

No sensible employer sets out to deliberately create an atmosphere of fear. It is rather the natural product of circumstances that invariably arises when an organization is too tightly controlled. In such circumstances, management imposes strict controls on risk taking and costs, which increase the level of scrutiny under which employees operate. The fear of failure pervades such an organization. The employee is put under

AN ORGANIZATION THAT IS FREED FROM THE SHACKLES OF FEAR RELISHES A CHALLENGE

pressure to minimize risk and control costs. Imposition by management of such a regime is rational behavior and cannot be described in isolation as anything other than prudent. The effect, however, is to set in motion a downward spiral of oppressiveness, which renders the employee fearful of every decision that needs to be taken.

Leadership style is also a key factor in determining the level of fear within an organization. Many organizational leaders conflate the imposition of fear with strength. Such leaders are often remote, unapproachable, and by their demeanor, intensify the pressure on subordinates to succeed. Leaders of this ilk often take the failure of employees as a personal affront and cannot see beyond how it will affect themselves. This style of leadership is perceived by others within the organization as the norm and will, almost certainly, be aped by other managers at all levels. Thus, the spiral of fear and oppressiveness takes another turn, stifling both individual and collective creativity and growth. It never seems to occur to those who act in this manner that real strength of leadership is demonstrated by having the strategic vision, and confidence, to allow room for employees to express themselves and utilize their talents to improve operational efficiency and create growth. Or does it occur to them that to lead through compassion, and earned respect, is a far more powerful and effective strategy than leading through oppression and fear.

Employees who are subjected to such an oppressive and fearful regime are afraid in many respects: they fear they will be reprimanded or subject to sanction if a mistake is made; they are constantly constrained in their actions for fear of how management will perceive those actions; they are afraid of how their colleagues will judge them if an error, or miscalculation, is made; they are afraid to think laterally and creatively and to go beyond their remit in respect of improving their operational efficiency or in dealing with arising difficulties.

Most employees will have a degree of authority residing in their functional remit. However, in an organization that is riddled with fear and oppression, employees are often reluctant to use this authority. This severely constrains operational efficiency.

The debilitating effect of fear on organizational output can be colossal. The tangible loss is, quite literally, immeasurable. It is not until these fears are removed, and entrenched conservatism is reversed, that an organization's released creative and innovative ambition gives an indication of the degree to which fear was impeding the organization.

The Removal of Fear

The Empowerment Paradigm allows an organization to cast off the shackles of fear and realize the full potential of its employees.

Fear is a deep-seated emotion that is difficult to eradicate. It requires vision, dedication, and a relentless focus to remove it completely from the workplace. However, once removed, the results are spectacular. It is difficult to overstate the positive effect on individual and collective morale, confidence, and general performance. The transformation is a joy to behold and makes the efforts involved well worthwhile. The benefits are also self-perpetuating, whereby the effects of removing fear empower the individual and collective aspirations of an organization to constantly strive to improve further.

Imagine, for a moment, the transformative effects of removing fear from the workplace. As an example, let us look at people working with functional authority within a medium-sized organization. These persons understand their role in the organization thoroughly and have acquired knowledge beyond their remit that can improve their functional efficiency. Do the employees pursue this and raise it as a suggestion with others within the organization? Consider how the employees would feel in an organization where management has imposed strictures, which forbid any deviation from the norm, where new ideas and innovation are frowned upon and considered risky, where to speak out is to risk the ire and ridicule of management and colleagues. Would these operatives feel confident enough to put forward these ideas to management? Would they not fear the reaction of management and colleagues? Would they have the inner belief that they could stray outside of their brief to suggest an improvement? In a fear-filled workplace, it is doubtful that they would. Then imagine the same employees placed in a fear-free environment where individual creativity and innovation is encouraged, lauded, and rewarded; where all new ideas are welcomed and listened to; where to speak out is not be disparaged but praised. Would the employees pursue their idea in these circumstances? The answer must surely be a resounding yes.

When examined in this way, it is obvious that removing fear from any organization will confer considerable advantages. These can be grouped into four categories: direct effects, secondary effects, information flow effects, and morale effects.

Direct Effects

These are the immediately tangible consequences of removing fear from the workplace and include the following:

> ## FEWER NONCONFORMITIES AND CORRECTIVE ACTIONS
>
> Fewer mistakes and greater accuracy of work from liberated employees

> ## IMPROVED QUALITY OF SUPPLY
>
> Improved organizational morale enhances desire to give customers the best

> ## REDUCED COSTS
>
> Confident employees encouraged to propose cost-saving measures

Secondary Effects

These are the less tangible but no less immediate consequences that flow from the removal of fear in the workplace and include the following:

> ## IMPROVED OPERATIONAL EFFICIENCY
>
> Attained through the release of innovation and improved practices

> ## INCREASED PRODUCTIVITY
>
> Contented employees are motivated to succeed

> ## REDUCED STAFF TURNOVER
>
> Happy employees don't want to leave

Information Flow Effects

These are the secondary effects of removing fear that dramatically improve the flow of information throughout an organization and include the following:

IMPROVED TRANSFER OF SKILLS AND KNOW-HOW

Employees able to communicate with colleagues and pass on knowledge and skills without reservation or fear of undermining their own position

IMPROVED INTRACOMPANY COMMUNICATION

Removal of fear-induced barriers enables information to flow

Morale Effects

These are the longer-term effects upon the self-esteem of the employee and collective morale of the organization. They include the following:

IMPROVED INDIVIDUAL AND COLLECTIVE MORALE

Self-confidence restored and renewed shared belief in organizational ability

IMPROVED INTRACOMPANY COMMUNICATION

Contented, confident employees communicating well with management reduces disputes.

An organization, which is freed from the shackles of fear, is one that is capable of taking necessary, calculated corporate risks. It is one that relishes a challenge and is prepared to push itself to improve and expand its supply portfolio while meeting the highest standards of quality and service. In contrast, an organization that refuses to push itself and declines all risks in the name of prudence and conservatism is one that loses the opportunity to expand and improve.

So how is a fear-free working environment created? There is no one-size-fits-all solution, but there are two basic principles that apply in all cases. Firstly, employees must understand that they are *trusted* and, secondly, that they are *valued*.

Employees who are trusted and valued will almost certainly develop a greater sense of self-esteem, which in turn engender within them the confidence to take on work outside of their usual remit and so increase productivity. This axiom is central to ensuring proper implementation of the Empowerment Paradigm methodology. Trust is a direct product of removing fear. Value flows from allowing the employees to use that freedom to express themselves through creativity and innovation. Trust and value, together, empower employees to be the best that they can be.

This may be achieved in differing ways, but some examples are set out below.

Trust Employees to Do Their Job

This might seem obvious, but an unchecked bureaucracy can easily trample upon this simplest of edicts.

Each employee will have had their authority and responsibilities set out in a job description. They will understand these to be the minimum expected of them.

> IN SHORT, TRUST EMPLOYEES TO DO THE JOB THEY WERE HIRED FOR.

For new employees, who have been carefully selected by way of a thorough recruitment process, it starts on the first day of their time within the organization. As such, although new recruits will, initially, be subject to an enhanced level of scrutiny during a probationary period, this will take the form of a constructive mentoring process rather than intrusive monitoring. It is crucial that time is taken to thoroughly induct new recruits into the organizational ethos. They must be told that they are trusted, not only to perform their function, but are also trusted, and actively encouraged and motivated, by the organization to expand their horizons by taking on new roles and functions within the organization. Over time, these new recruits will come to the full understanding that such personal aspiration and growth are not only actively encouraged but also expected. This policy will increase the multifunctionality of the workforce, simplify function, and enhance operational efficiency.

A significant proportion of new recruits will be in first-time employment. This should be seen by the organization as an opportunity to ensure that the principles of the Empowerment Paradigm are thoroughly inculcated, without the distraction of preconceived expectations imparted by other organizations. Such employees should be nurtured and will, in time, exhibit the purest, and fullest, expression of the methodology.

IT IS DIFFICULT TO OVERSTATE THE POSITIVE EFFECT ON INDIVIDUAL AND COLLECTIVE MORALE, CONFIDENCE, AND GENERAL PERFORMANCE.

Experienced employees, who have been performing their tasks for years, must also understand that to transfer their own skills and know-how to new recruits is to increase the collective knowledge of the organization and should be welcomed rather than feared. Concentration of knowledge creates bottlenecks and barriers, which in turn lead to misunderstandings and insecurity. All employees must be made to understand that sharing knowledge does not diminish the individual but, rather, elevates the organization's collective ability to improve, innovate, and ultimately succeed. In this way, all employees, including those holding crucial skills and expertise, are able to optimize opportunity and growth for themselves and the organization.

Many employees will have been performing their tasks for years. Accordingly, they can perform their tasks without intrusive regulation and management constantly peering over their shoulder. Instead, management must ensure employees, at all levels, know that they are trusted in terms of their skill, knowledge, and capability to perform their tasks to the best of their ability and to become the best that they can be. This trust should extend to all employees being encouraged by management to push themselves to increase, and transfer, their knowledge and skill in order to optimize the quality and output of their function, and the organization as a whole. Accordingly, management must make themselves intimately familiar with each employee's duties in order to offer guidance to employees to optimize their function in a manner that is realistically attainable.

> SHARING KNOWLEDGE DOES NOT DIMINISH THE INDIVIDUAL.

When employees are successful in achieving an improvement in their function, management should express its appreciation to the employee immediately, whatever the increment of that improvement.

Many organizations hire temporary staff in times of high demand so as to avoid increased overheads and eliminate layoff costs when demand decreases. Temporary employees should be integrated into project teams with permanent project team members taking responsibility for temporary employees' performance of the assigned project function. Proper incentives set for project performance will ensure that permanent project team members understand the importance of the collective project output and can be trusted to ensure temporary employees do not fail in their function.

In short, trust employees to do the job they were hired for. Encourage and expect improvements in that job function. Motivate the desire to increase skills and to take on more responsibilities and new roles and to transfer knowledge and skills to other employees.

Employees who are incapable in this regard will have been moved to areas matching their level of competence or, otherwise, let go.

Removing Unnecessary Layers of Management

A natural consequence of successfully implementing the Empowerment Paradigm is a confident workforce that renders unnecessary layers of management redundant, and so reduces costs and enhances profitability.

Employees working within a fear-free environment, with a skill mix and confidence to work autonomously, do not require constant supervision.

Freedom to move beyond its functional remit and encouragement to acquire and use multifunctional skills allow an organization, if it so wishes, to dispense with functionally oriented departments and departmental management, which can act as bureaucratic deadweights, blunting creativity and innovation. By switching to a contract-focused rather than a department-focused organization, team members report to a team leader. This automatically resolves the dichotomy of hierarchical reporting, which exists when multifunctional employees operate within a departmentally focused organization.

The Empowerment Paradigm allows organizations to reorientate and to focus upon delivery and profitability. Take an organization that specializes in turnkey contracts. The key focus for this organization is contract execution. The Empowerment Paradigm methodologies allow this organization to invest its energies in the contract via team leaders who are able to draw directly upon a pool of employees to meet all contract functions and requirements. In such an organization, there is no need for functional departmental managers. The team leaders fulfill the departmental manager role. Contract-focused operations are less bureaucratic, less costly, more directly accountable to the revenue stream, dealing more flexibly with problems arising, and better in serving the customer.

By removing unnecessary levels of management and departmental structures, authority is devolved to those who perform the work, thereby enhancing the confidence and dynamics of the workforce and increasing operational efficiency.

Responsibility and Accountability

A corollary to the principle of trusting employees to do their job is the increased responsibility this brings and the value that a corresponding level of accountability confers throughout an organization. Conferring appropriate levels of responsibility and accountability is another axiom that is fundamental to the success of the Empowerment Paradigm.

Giving employees the support and confidence to take on more responsibilities for their function and even to reach beyond their remit allow an organization to make that employee directly accountable for their existing, or expanded, role. Moreover, it is a demonstration of the organization's trust in its employees, which is transformative in its effect on individual and collective confidence and morale, and brings employees at all levels closer to the organizational purpose and goals.

EMPLOYEES WHO ARE ACCOUNTABLE FOR THE PERFORMANCE OF THEIR REMIT TAKE A GREATER INTEREST IN THE OUTCOMES.

As is shown repeatedly in the proceeding chapters, transferring responsibility and accountability to those employees tasked with managing a contract (let us call them team leaders or project managers) devolves and incentivizes contract execution. In this way, those closest to the day-to-day execution of all contract functions, and so best placed to know what is needed to serve the contract, are empowered to take decisions, which optimize contract performance and margins. Making these team leaders accountable for contract budgets, schedules, and margins ensures that on-time delivery and profitability remain the primary focus of the contract. This contrasts starkly with organizations who fail to devolve responsibility and accountability to team leaders and so allow contract objectives to conflict with one another. For example, making a team leader responsible for on-time delivery without ceding responsibility for project expenditure can result in a conflict between that team leader and the organization's financial controller.

Employees who are accountable for the performance of their remit take a greater interest in the outcomes. For example, a team leader who is directly accountable for a contract's bottom line will take a greater interest in all aspects of contract expenditure. This extends from man-hours spent to the grade of hotel used during a customer visit. Moreover, the same team leader will resist unnecessary managerial interference that increases costs.

Empowered team leaders and their team members will have clear objectives and a sense of purpose that are often missing in organizations that retain power in the echelons of senior management. Team leaders and team members who are trusted in this way reward the organization by exhibiting a drive to succeed, which requires little oversight, or input, from senior management.

Dealing with Mistakes and Transgressions

Employing the principles of the Empowerment Paradigm allows, as detailed above, for improved relations among employees, and between management and subordinates.

> MANY PROBLEMS CAN BE RESOLVED WITHIN A PEER GROUP MORE QUICKLY AND EFFICIENTLY THAN WITH MANAGEMENT INTERVENTION.

This should not mean that there is a lax attitude to discipline. Transgressions or mistakes have to be addressed. However, in accordance with the core values of the Empowerment Paradigm, these matters should be addressed constructively, transparently, and in a way that is not demotivational or does not cause fear within the workplace.

Anyone can make a mistake. Management should ensure that any chastisement is appropriate, proportional, involves a measure of understanding, and that help is offered to the employee(s) involved. The employees must feel that they are learning from the process of resolving their mistakes and understand that their mistakes are addressed by management constructively and sympathetically. In this way, employees are encouraged to volunteer the disclosure of mistakes when they are made, allowing earlier intervention and mitigation and so reduce risk and exposure. Responding with anger or severe chastisement, to mistakes, will have the opposite effect. Instead, management should adopt an attitude that leads employees to feel they are being helped to resolve the mistake and that steps are taken to ensure it will not happen again. This, in turn, will lessen the instinctive human tendency to proclaim "It's not my fault" when a mistake is made and will smoothen and shorten the resolution and necessary learning process. Employees should be made to understand that the resolution process in dealing with mistakes is a learning process, which benefits the organization as a whole by identifying the root cause of problems and ensuring that these are communicated to others within the organization. As such, the resolution process should be seen as a natural organizational function to which no individual blame is attached and which increases the organization's collective knowledge.

Dealing with transgressions can be more problematic. Rules must been seen to be applied evenhandedly throughout the organization. No one can be seen to operate outside of the organizational rules. Disciplinary procedures will allow for dispassionate and fair application of punishments. However, discipline should be dispensed in a way that does not cause undue embarrassment to those involved, puts the issue behind all those involved, and where possible, makes the details known to employees so that fairness can be seen to have been done and rumors of unfair treatment can be quashed.

Use the Right Quality Management System

Using the correct quality management system is vital to empowering the individual employee and allowing collective organizational coherence.

A TAILOR-MADE, QUALITY MANAGEMENT SYSTEM THAT SERVES THE ORGANIZATION MUST ALLOW INNOVATION AND CREATIVITY.

It is common for quality management systems to constrain and dictate organizational function. This occurs mainly as a result of organizations paying only lip service to quality in order to meet standards, which may be a prerequisite to bidding with certain customers, or only complying fully with the quality regime a short while before a scheduled quality audit. In these circumstances, management invariably uses off-the-shelf quality management systems. This one-size-fits-all approach is ultimately self-defeating and costly.

Organizations that adopt this easy and half-hearted approach to quality often find that difficulties arise for no particular reason and are problematic to identify and resolve. Invariably, the cause is a quality procedure that fails to properly take account of the functional requirements of an organization, particularly when defects occur or changes are required. Such procedural indigestion is a common complaint of ill-fitting and poorly-installed quality management systems.

This does not mean that an organization should employ expensive consultants to install a quality management system. In many cases, it is such consultants, who do not fully understand the organizational function and who have a vested interest in using a generic system, that seem to delight in overcomplication and exemplify, and exacerbate, the phenomenon of using the wrong quality management system.

The quality management system should be designed by those who understand the function of the organization intimately, and should evolve through the input of employees via the intrinsic mechanisms of the system: management review, internal audits, non-conformities, and corrective actions.

The quality management system should accurately reflect the function of the organization. It should be tailor-made in order to serve the organization by minimizing expensive nonconformities and corrective actions, as well as facilitating necessary change in nondisruptive and economical manner. It should not straightjacket the organizational function. In other words, the tail should not wag the dog.

A quality management system that dictates a change in function, but does not lead to a simplification of that function or an improvement in quality, is not working in the best interests of an organization.

A tailor-made quality management system that serves the organization must allow innovation and creativity to result in positive changes. It must never stifle these instincts by imposing unnecessary procedural constraints.

It is, therefore, important that senior management commit to using a bespoke quality management system with constructive and instructive quality procedures, which allow employees the opportunity to make a contribution to improve the organizational function, just as a manager should never shut down an employee's idea when brought to them, so the quality management system should not do so procedurally. Of equal importance is the need to periodically review the quality management system to ensure that it remains fit-for-purpose, particularly, when a change is made to organizational structure or function.

A vital element of an organization's quality management system, in the context of the Empowerment Paradigm, is for the responsible and accountable managers to evaluate their own operational remit. In the case of team leaders, nonconformities must be assessed in terms of severity and cost and corrective actions formulated in conjunction with other team leaders. Nonconformities of a generic nature, along with a proven corrected action, must be communicated to other team leaders and team members. This ensures mistakes are not repeated from contract to contract and that corrective actions become common organizational property. This principle of evaluating and correcting deficiencies in their own organizational remit extends to all levels and all functions: from senior management to team members, from the sales and proposals function to administrative support.

Promote Communication and Value Ideas and Innovation

Communication is vital in all organizations, and good communications should be promoted as a matter of course. Employees should not feel constrained in raising concerns and making suggestions. Indeed, this should be actively encouraged.

In order to facilitate good communications, management, to the highest levels, should operate an open-door policy, clearly stating that they are prepared to listen to what the individual employee has to say. Management should always make themselves available to deal with an issue raised by an employee at short notice. This engenders a sense of worth within the employee, as well as expeditiously addresses problems that are a potential impediment to operational efficiency. Management should also go to great lengths to ensure that they actively seek to unearth hidden or unreported problems, properly understand any problems brought to them, empathize with the employee, praise the employee for raising the issue, and participate fully in the resolution.

> IDEAS ARE WELCOMED, AND SO THE FLOW OF IDEAS CONTINUES.

Management, again to the highest levels, should elicit regular informal contact with all levels of the organization, creating a basic level of trust and so ensuring that all employees feel comfortable in communicating with management. Senior management should make an effort to remember employee names and personal circumstances. It is amazing how motivating this can be. In this way, the highest echelons of an organization can discreetly identify problems at even the lowest levels.

Communication among employees is also of great importance. This communication becomes most effective when employees implicitly trust one another and know each other well, both professionally and socially. Such natural relationships lead to an ease of working that facilitates the flow of knowledge laterally (including new ideas) throughout an organization, and improvements can be self-perpetuating

NO IDEA SHOULD EVER BE DISMISSED OUT OF HAND.

via constructive intraorganizational competition. For example, an employee, seeing a colleague make an improvement in function, may adopt the same, or similar, idea to improve their own function or may even be inspired to improve upon their colleague's idea. These horizontal communication channels also help employees identify any problem that colleagues may be experiencing or afford them the confidence to reach out for help from, or offer help to, their peers without fear of diminishing their own status. Accordingly, many problems can be resolved within a peer group more quickly and efficiently than with management intervention.

Ideas and innovation should be actively encouraged from all employees. This may be promoted by monthly prizes awarded by the CEO.

In particular, employees should be made to understand that the organization welcomes suggestions to make operations quicker, cheaper, and more efficient. An employee should not be constrained, in any way, from making suggestions about matters outside of their functional remit.

Management must ensure that all suggestions are valued and should receive an acknowledgment, if only verbal, but never simply ignored.

> EMPLOYEES SHOULD BE LISTENED TO, TREATED WITH RESPECT, AND THEIR IDEAS TAKEN SERIOUSLY.

This is a vital part of releasing the talent of employees. No idea should ever be dismissed out of hand. All should be considered and welcomed equally. It is more than likely that many of these ideas are flawed and have little, if any, merit. But some could be brilliant innovations. But how, I hear you ask, do I deal with all these ideas? Surely they are an unnecessary distraction. This is where discipline and diplomatic management is required. Let us take another example. We all know certain employees who have an opinion about everything and are not shy in propagating them. Let's say that one such employee is dominating a meeting and has a suggestion to make about all agenda items, including those outside of their remit. The instinctive reaction would be to shut that person down, but this is contrary to the principles of the Empowerment Paradigm and should never, ever happen. Rather, in these circumstances, the employee should be praised, thanked for their suggestions, and asked to see a designated person (or task force) outside of the meeting to pursue the issues. In this way, all at the meeting will understand, demonstrably, that new ideas are welcomed, and so the flow of ideas continues. You may just strike lucky with the one that, with proper attention and application of resources, makes your organization's fortune.

It is a truism that those who are bubbling over with ideas are often, but not always, those with the most talent. They are often egregiously extravert and feel no embarrassment about the ideas they are propagating or how they are perceived by colleagues. These employees should be listened to, treated with respect, and their ideas taken seriously, and supported when the ideas seem viable. It will not take long to identify those with real talent as opposed to those who just have too much to say of themselves. It is vital that managers do not shut these employees down because they create additional work or because of professional jealousy.

Periodic in-house newsletters are a good way of improving communication and ensuring that employees understand that all ideas and innovations are welcomed, listened to, and are seen to be valued.

Social interaction and team building are covered in more detail elsewhere, but it is vital to understand that employees need to develop mutual respect and a keen social and professional empathy, which enable them to trust and support each other, both in the workplace and in their private lives if required.

Communicating Organizational Status

One of the greatest sources of fear within an organization is starving employees of information with respect to current financial status, prospects, and impending organizational change.

Employees will generally have a sense of what is happening but will not know for sure. This uncertainty generates fear and lack of confidence. Employees are considerably more engaged in their work and wedded to organizational purpose and goals when they are periodically appraised, in general terms, of financial status, prospects, and planned changes.

ANY CHANGES TO THE ORGANIZATION OR POLICY MUST ALSO BE CLEARLY AND PROMPTLY COMMUNICATED.

Communication in this regard may be achieved in memoranda or a short statement at a social gathering. Such opportunities may also be used to elicit support and exhort employees to greater efforts.

Communicating organizational status and plans also allows senior management to set and communicate short-, medium-, and long-term organizational objectives. In particular, it affords senior management an opportunity to fine-tune short-term efforts. This may include extolling employees to make an extra effort in a particular direction; passing on to designers a particular market demand; requesting suggestions for product improvements or new products; ensuring employees, at all levels, understand what is required of them to remain successful or improve the level of success; ensuring acquired knowledge is thoroughly inculcated at all levels of the organization.

An employee's fear of losing their job is an entirely rational fear. One way of alleviating this fear is to ensure that during busy periods, activities are outsourced and taken in-house during quiet periods. Employees should understand this and see it as a buffer against job losses. This will require contracts with outsource vendors to be flexible.

UNCERTAINTY GENERATES A LACK OF CONFIDENCE AND FEAR.

Any changes to the organization, or policy, must also be clearly, and promptly, communicated to employees. This includes changes in personnel, anticipated changes in workload levels, advice on award of contracts or loss of the same, and structural reorganization.

Transparent management, committed to clear and honest disclosure, creates the stability employees need to perform their work, sure in the organizational purpose and goals and unencumbered with fears for their future.

Career Path and Personal Growth

It is important that time is taken to thoroughly induct new employees, ensuring that they fully understand the organizational ethos and the numerous opportunities available to advance their careers. This assists integration and ensures all new recruits are motivated to make the fullest contribution from the start. This is particularly effective if conducted by the CEO or other senior manager. The new recruits will then understand from day 1 that they are a vital operational component and have prospects for advancement.

> ENABLE ALL EMPLOYEES TO DO WHAT THEY KNOW BEST OR PROGRESS TO WHERE THEIR TALENTS AND ASPIRATIONS LIE.

New recruits should be given responsibility at the earliest possible stage. This optimizes the use of human resources, gives an employee an earlier opportunity to prove their worth, and accelerates their path along the learning curve. For example, an inexperienced project manager should be allowed to visit a customer on their own and without technical backup. This allows the project manager the maximum opportunity to learn through autonomously addressing the customer's needs. Any queries that cannot be answered contemporaneously may be dealt with at a later stage. This freedom to operate autonomously, without fear, epitomizes the methodology of the Empowerment Paradigm.

Each employee should be made to understand that the organization encourages ambition and personal growth.

All employees should be made aware that they are expected to set a career path with defined improvement objectives. Such objectives should be consistent with the organization's philosophy to promote self-improvement and to enable all employees to do what they know best or progress to where their talents and aspirations lie. This allows employees the fullest opportunity to become the best that they can. It includes permitting the acquisition of skills to move outside of the employees' existing functional remit and allowing them to aspire to reach to the highest levels within the organization. Attaining multifunctionality is a valuable tool for an organization and employees should be urged to acquire such status and to understand that the organization values this and that they will be rewarded for making efforts in this regard.

Management should also ensure that employees understand that they are exhorted to think laterally, to want to take on more responsibilities, and to move into other areas of the organization. This ensures talent moves freely within the organization and enables each employee to find their most rewarding, and effective, niche and most comfortable hierarchical level.

From time to time, the CEO, or a member of senior management, will sit with the employee and discuss their career-path objectives, ensuring support is offered and advice given if sought. Actions on the part of the organization and employee should be agreed and considered as informal contracts to realize the potential of the individual.

In short, the organization should ensure that employees understand that they are urged to be the best, and most effective, that they can be.

Recognizing and Rewarding Service and Excellence

All employees should be immediately praised and thanked for their contribution to the organization, for improvements made or suggested. They must also be informed when performance is less than satisfactory. In this way, the employee clearly, and contemporaneously, understands when they have made a positive contribution or the reverse. There is little point in informing employees that

> PRAISE AND GRATITUDE ARE MOTIVATIONALLY MOST EFFECTIVE WHEN GIVEN AT THE TIME OF THE DEED.

they have not performed well six months earlier at a salary review meeting. Conversely, praise and gratitude is motivationally most effective when given at the time of the deed.

Accordingly, employees do not have to guess how senior management feels about their performance. They will automatically know this because they will effectively be stakeholders in the organization, whereby positive contributions are guaranteed to be financially rewarded when the organization prospers.

When performance is not as required and expected by the organization, the employees must be assisted by management to improve their performance.

In order to stimulate extraordinary performance, most organizations operate a bonus-reward scheme. In the Empowerment Paradigm, such schemes should be inclusive by recognizing excellence in non-sales-related functions, as well as direct revenue-generating functions. If the Empowerment Paradigm is working well, all employees within the organization shall be worthy of a bonus. If they are not, then they should not be an employee of the organization. Fully inclusive bonus schemes of this type work well in that all employees have a stake in the bottom line and become involved in ensuring their peers are performing their own roles correctly and exhort them to greater efforts to maximize profitability (and bonus levels).

Employees should be valued, not just in their direct contribution, but also in terms of the length of service to the organization. This need only be a notional reward, but it augments other measures designed to show the worth the organization attaches to each individual.

Harnessing the Individual Competitive Instinct

Human beings work well together in packs. This is why team building is relatively easy within well-run organizations. However, an employee's prime pack is invariably the family. In this regard, the organization's needs are secondary to the family's needs. Within the workplace, this manifests itself in the need for an employee to excel and so maximize status and income. All organizations will recognize the individual competitive instinct and indeed, many will seek to encourage this.

A wise organization understands that to allow the individual competitive instinct to remain unchecked is wasteful and disruptive. Organizations must, therefore, seek to harness this individual competitive instinct to the collective good.

Organizational leadership is vital in this regard. As explored in chapter 3, an organization's values help define the relationship among employees. These should promote mutual respect, collective responsibility, the free exchange of information and knowledge, empathy, and support.

Employees should understand that their individual endeavors and successes will be rewarded but that it is organizational success that is paramount. Those seeking advancement through subversive means should find themselves at odds with other team members and senior management, who understand that such behavior is counterproductive in terms of morale, levels of productivity, and collective success.

Success in others should be lauded by colleagues who understand that their own fortunes are tied to this.

In short, an organization must harness the individual competitive instinct to drive collective success, ensuring that all employees are incentivized to achieve this through team work, the free exchange of knowledge, and mutual respect.

Social Interaction

The primary instinct to support the family is examined above. Nearly all employees have families who compete with the organization for their time. The organization should make efforts to understand these conflicting demands by involving families in social activities so the family members come to understand the organization's ethos and the requirements placed upon employees.

> MAKE EFFORTS TO UNDERSTAND THOSE CONFLICTING DEMANDS BY INVOLVING FAMILY MEMBERS IN SOCIAL ACTIVITIES.

This policy can be carried through summer jobs programs, in which family members are prioritized, to the better understanding of the organization's work environment, pressures, and demands.

Social relationships forged between spouses and partners are particularly useful in improving mutual respect and empathy among employees, which lead to enhanced working relations within the workplace. This can be an invaluable support mechanism for employees in times of great need. The support, both financially and emotionally, of colleagues during bereavements and other personal traumas transcends the organizational imperative, but as a by-product, it serves to bind the employees' working community and their families together in a powerful and enduring way. The following is a true-life illustration: an employee in a regional fabrication plant of organization lost his wife and possessions in a house fire. He was uninsured. The organization had been operating according to the principles of the Empowerment Paradigm for several years. When the news reached the head office of the organization, without prompting from management, employees started a fund to financially assist the employee. Donations were sought throughout the organization and a substantial amount was raised. The CEO then announced that the organization would match the donations and so doubled the fund. In the years that followed, whenever the CEO visited the fabrication facility, that employee would approach the CEO and offer his continuing thanks for the help received. This is a powerful example of how social interaction and empathy has flourished within a working environment that is free of the constraints of fear and negative competitive rivalry, which allows compassion toward colleagues to thrive. It also reinforces the employee's understanding that the organization is always there to help in whatever the circumstances.

Community programs and charitable giving are equally powerful ways of promoting collective well-being and cohesiveness. The power of giving to others is remarkably rewarding. It allows employees to feel good about themselves and enhances the image of the organization within the community. For example, employees may decide, collectively, to forego a Christmas party or corporate gift in lieu of the organization donating an equal sum to a local charity. The organization should not dictate such a policy but ensure that such arrangements are permissible. Employees should be allowed to organize the details and present this to the management. In recognition of the collective sacrifice, the organization might make an additional donation on top of the in lieu amount.

Chapter Three

Establishing the Credo

The Vision Thing

An organization must establish a credo by which to operate and judge its performance and ethics. This is usually encapsulated with the organizational *vision*, *mission*, and *values*.

An organization without a vision is an organization without a future. A vision illuminates the path to prosperity and success. Without it, an organization is doomed to repeat its mistakes and entrench its failures.

A *vision statement* should afford all members of an organization an inspirational focus, allowing them to entwine their personal aspirations with collective organizational goals. It should say, "Join us on this journey, and you will personally prosper."

> AN ORGANIZATION WITHOUT A VISION IS AN ORGANIZATION WITHOUT A FUTURE.

A *mission statement* sits beneath the vision and should set out, in broad terms, how an organization can achieve its vision.

Underpinning the vision and mission are a set of *values* by which an organization functions. These values, in essence, represent the principles by which an organization should operate. It is through these values that the doctrine of the Empowerment Paradigm can be propagated throughout an organization. These values ensure that all employees, at all levels, are able to trust each other; prescribe the ideals by which the organization operates; promote honesty, respect, integrity, and compassion; and mold the personality of the organization, how it perceives itself, and how it is regarded by others.

Operational Compatibility

An organization's vision, mission, and values are designed to guide and inspire. They are not intended to constrain an organization. As such, they should allow, and encourage, operational flexibility—promoting multifunctionality, innovation, and creativity within a fear-free environment.

Aim High, but Be Inclusive

The objectives set out within the vision, mission, and values must be ambitious enough to extend and challenge employees but not ridiculously high so as to act as a disincentive. Nothing is as rewarding as achieving a very ambitious target. But equally, little is more demoralizing than continually striving toward a target that is clearly beyond an organization's capability.

> NOTHING IS AS REWARDING AS ACHIEVING A VERY AMBITIOUS TARGET.

The vision, mission, and values must also be wide enough to ensure they are inclusive of the functions of all employees. There is little point in attempting to motivate an organization, en masse, when the guiding principles have no relevance to a large proportion of the workforce.

The vision, mission, and values should clearly define how employees are treated by the organization. In this way, employees will know that the organization will treat them fairly, nurture their talents, and help them meet their aspirations.

It is also important that the vision, mission, and values have relevance to matters outside the working environment. They should, therefore, include reference to family life and interaction with the local community.

Mean It, Believe It, Live It

Most modern organizations establish an ethos in the form of a written and posted statement of intent. This is usually framed and displayed in the foyer and maybe in the CEO's office. It is also most probably prominent on organizational sales literature. In fact, it is likely that the majority of employees walk past the statement every day of their working life, and just skip over it when it is appears in literature.

In most organizations, it is doubtful that any employee knows what is contained within the statement, let alone believes what is written and uses it as a guide to their working lives.

GOALS MUST COMPLEMENT RATHER THAN CONSTRAIN ORGANIZATIONAL OPERATION.

The Empowerment Paradigm requires an organization to become imbued with its vision, mission, and values.

The vision, mission, and values must be carefully formulated to reflect organizational goals and must complement rather than constrain organizational operation. They must have at heart the core principles of creating a fear-free workplace and empowerment of the individual to operate freely and to grow, create, and innovate to the betterment of the organization.

The vision, mission, and values should inspire employees to strive to become the best that they can be. Releasing an employee's spirit and determination to succeed affords them the confidence to take on greater responsibility and to become accountable for their actions. Accordingly, employees are actively involved in determining their own level

WITHOUT A FUTURE, ALL ORGANIZATIONS REVERT TO THE PAST.

of success and reward and know that this assures their future within the organizations.

It is vital that all employees who buy into these principles are allowed to contribute to the written statement over time. Accordingly, the organization must allow its guiding principles to evolve. Employees must understand that these are not imposed by management and that they are open to constructive challenge and may be adjusted when valid suggestions are received.

It is this inclusive, bottom-up approach that promotes a full understanding of where the organization is heading (*vision*), how it plans to get there (*mission*), and the manner in which it intends to travel (*values*).

In short, everyone should understand that the organization is not just paying lip service to some esoteric and remotely applicable ideology, but it is, instead, something that they mean and expect all employees to believe and live by.

Employees at all levels who have fully bought into the vision will strive to keep it alive, fresh, and vibrant. The CEO plays a vital role in this by reiterating the importance of the vision, which enshrines the organization's aspirations and ultimate destination. Without this vision, an organization has no future, and without a future, all organizations revert to the past.

This policy must be seen to apply to everyone within the organization. No one should be exempted, and management to the highest level must understand their vital role in leading by example.

It is important that customers see, and understand, that an organization is living by its stated principles. Management should ensure that customers understand this as part of the organization's marketing strategy.

The Power of Mantras

An organization's values are a guide as to how it should operate. They set a moral compass, which dictates the ethical policy of the organization and acceptable standards of behavior for all employees, at all levels. These are the day-to-day principles by which the organization judges itself.

It is useful to set, within these values, mantras that encapsulate the direction of operation. "Quality from the start," "Think what your customers need," "When there is a need, meet it," "Can I buy that cheaper?" are all examples of mantras that can have a powerful influence upon operational direction and efficiency.

The organization must carefully select several, but not too many, mantras that are key to its operational focus and direction. As part of the values, these mantras should be propagated throughout the organization and continually reinforced.

> MANTRAS ENCAPSULATE THE DIRECTION OF OPERATION.

Management should use these mantras when communicating with employees, either in conversation, or more formally, in writing. Employees will then understand that management is not just paying lip service to the mantras.

Employees should not feel embarrassed in using the mantras when communicating with colleagues. Indeed, mantras should enter the lexicon of everyday organizational dialogue.

However, as with all oft-repeated phrases, it is possible, over time, for that meaning to become diluted or lost. It is, therefore, important that management ensures that the true meaning of a mantra is understood by employees. This may be done in groups or individually. For example, the mantra "Quality from the start" should be actively and repeatedly assessed in the context of evaluating nonconformities. As described in chapter 2, nonconformities are assessed in terms of their impact and cost to the organization and corrective actions formulated and communicated throughout the organization. This allows employees to understand, in practical terms, the impact of not adhering to this mantra, ensuring the correct meaning is understood and misconceptions avoided.

Propagation and Reinforcement

Management must ensure that the message contained within the vision, mission, and values is constantly propagated and reinforced. This may be achieved in a number of ways.

Most simply, the vision, mission, and values must be included within an employee handbook. They must also feature centrally in the induction process.

> ENSURE THAT THE MESSAGE IS CONSTANTLY PROPAGATED AND REINFORCED.

Newsletters and speeches should invite employees to review their performance and to evaluate how they have stack up against the vision, mission, and values.

Employees may even be encouraged to contribute examples to newsletters or in meetings, with prizes awarded for the best by the CEO, on a regular basis. Employees may also be asked to nominate a fellow employee who has acted in a way exemplified these principles. This need not be a work-related activity as the vision, mission, and values will have been drawn widely to include interaction with family life and the local community.

These measures will ensure that everyone within the organization is persuaded by the merits of understanding, working, and living by the objectives and principles expounded by the vision, mission, and values.

Chapter Four

The Ubiquitous Leader

Leading by Example

As mentioned in chapter 2, the eradication of fear requires a multistranded approach with an underlying theme of ensuring all employees understand that they are *trusted* and *valued*.

A CEO WHO TAKES AN UNREMITTINGLY HANDS-ON APPROACH

The principles enshrined within the Empowerment Paradigm are at their most effective when they are wholeheartedly adopted and relentlessly propagated throughout the organization. A leader who is able to set a clear vision for the organization's future and takes an unremittingly hands-on approach to getting there can achieve this. Such a leader must become intimately involved in every particular aspect of driving through the strategy, becoming the Empowerment Paradigm's most ardent, and steadfast, advocate.

The behavior of the leader and the rapport they establish with the workforce are vital. The leader must ensure that they are respected and not feared. They must be seen as the rock upon which the security and stability of the organization is founded.

Employees must come to understand that the leader is transparent and honest, has compassion not only for them but for their family members, understands the demands of family commitments, sets realistic organizational goals and knows how to get there, makes available the full resources employees need to perform their jobs properly, offers the prospect of advancement, rewards success fairly, and ensures organizational stability and job security.

> THE CEO MUST ALSO CONNECT WITH EMPLOYEES WHEN THEY COMMUNICATE THEIR VISION AND DIRECTION OF TRAVEL.

The leader must be steadfast and committed to the organizational vision and ensure that employees understand that they will not waver in this respect. The leader must also connect with employees when communicating their vision and direction of travel. Employees must buy into this completely and be willing to trust their leader and loyally follow even in uncertain times and circumstances. The objective is for employees to listen to the leader extol the organizational vision and how it is going to get there and respond by saying, or thinking, "Yes! I get it. This is how I can secure my own future and success."

A leader who is optimistic and reacts positively and constructively to all circumstances inspires all others within an organization to behave similarly and so imbues the entire organization with the right frame of mind to meet the challenges that will arise on a regular basis. The enthusiasm of a committed leader is also contagious and can break down hierarchical and social barriers, which often intensify and entrench inherent insecurities. These insecurities are at the root of workplace fear.

The power of positive thinking is a powerful leadership tool. The leader must enthusiastically support the goals of an organization and, as described in the preceding chapter, ensure these are sufficiently ambitious so as to properly stretch the organization. By constantly reinforcing the belief that such ambitious goals can be attained, the leader will ensure that employees also believe in these goals. It is amazing how often such seemingly impossible goals are met when an organization wholeheartedly adopts such an attitude.

Unless blessed with a naturally charismatic personality, it may be difficult to achieve the above. This chapter shows how this may be achieved: by examining how a leader can lead an organization to shed its insecurities, attaining a collective maturity and confidence, which permeates to the lowest levels and culminates in enhanced commercial success.

The Inertia of Status Quo

Getting started is often difficult. It takes courage and commitment to decide to challenge the existing state of affairs.

> IT TAKES COURAGE AND COMMITMENT TO DECIDE TO CHALLENGE THE EXISTING STATE OF AFFAIRS.

The first hurdle is for the leader to take a decision to implement the changes required. This includes setting the vision, mission, and values as described in the previous chapter. It also involves establishing a product/service portfolio, dictates which markets to target, and explains exactly what is required from the workforce.

The second hurdle is to convince those in senior positions that such change is both necessary and desirable. In other words, ensure that they buy into and are equally committed to the vision and direction/method of travel. It is vital that efforts are not undermined by those with a different agenda.

The third, and most vital, hurdle is to convince employees to embrace the opportunities and rewards offered to them by committing to implement the Empowerment Paradigm.

The appeal of the Empowerment Paradigm is that when explained, who can reasonably object? Who doesn't want a contented, confident, motivated, innovative workforce? Who can object to improved internal communication and constructive and empathetic social interaction? Surely, everyone will want a greater role in determining their own future security and level of reward.

This is where the creed of the ubiquitous leader comes to the fore.

All employees should see that the leader is actively involved in and offers compassionate and unwavering support for all functions of the organization, asking if there are problems, assisting in resolution, getting to know employees' names, and coming to understand employees' work and social circumstances.

In short, the leader should be committed to being there to support employees, show them they are *valued*, and gain their *trust*. The leader should try not to delegate problems. The leader must let employees see that their leader is taking the time to personally help in resolving even minor problems. This includes direct and transparent communication of all matters that impact upon employees' operations and well-being. Employees must come to explicitly trust all that they are told and understand that there are no hidden agenda or withheld facts that jeopardize their security and ability to succeed. This is vital to ensuring the complete freedom of employees to create and innovate.

This trust is not easy to imbue. It must be earned and will be hard won. But such endeavors will, ultimately, reap rewards that far outstrip the effort involved.

Extolling the Credo

> EMPLOYEES NEED TO KNOW WHERE THEY ARE BEING LED AND WHAT'S IN IT FOR THEM.

The leader must involve themselves in all aspects of communicating the organization's defined vision, mission, and values. As explained in the preceding chapter, it is within its values that the soul of an organization resides.

Employees need to know where they are being led and what's in it for them. The leader must lead by constantly reinforcing and explaining the virtues of the message contained within the vision, mission, and values. In this way, employees gain an insight into how they can best contribute to improve the organization.

Just as an organization with no vision has no future, a leader who fails to clearly and firmly define the direction of travel is no true leader. A true-life example is this: a company is investing heavily in a new product line, which has good prospects for commercial success. The leader does not believe the product is viable and tells the organization's development team, who have invested much time and money in the new product line, that there is no real prospect of commercial success.

However, the leader, hedging their bets and showing a distinct lack of courage, does not close down the work on the project. Apart from being highly demotivational, this sends a message of ambivalence to the team and singularly fails to set a direction of travel. Such behavior from a leader is inexcusable.

By taking a personal hand in propagating this message, the leader is telling, and showing, all employees that he believes in the message, is committed to it, and lives by it. This personal approach by the head of an organization also informs the employee that they are worthy of consideration and increases self-esteem.

Here, There, and Everywhere

The leader must try to be ubiquitous by staying physically close to all functional operations and imparting a consistent and unwavering message. They must speak to employees at all levels of the organization in a plain and friendly way that is free of condescension. The employee must be made to feel comfortable so as to promote discourse. Through this discourse, as examined in previous chapters, employees are encouraged to come up with new ideas and to generally innovate. It is vital

> STAYING PHYSICALLY CLOSE TO ALL FUNCTIONAL OPERATIONS AND IMPARTING A CONSISTENT AND UNWAVERING MESSAGE

that the leader listens earnestly to these ideas and has the courage and humility to incorporate those ideas that improve operational efficiency and the prospects of the organization. It is equally important that the leader personally, and openly, gives credit for those ideas. This encourages others to come forward and will ensure that the organization's operations are fluid and constantly in search of improvement.

When visiting organizational locations outside of the head office, the leader should ensure that they talk to employees throughout the locations. For example, if visiting a fabrication shop, don't just sit in the office with the shop manager and leave. Instead, take time to talk, and listen, to administrative and shop floor employees.

The leader must try to attend all organizational social events if only for a limited period. A short motivational speech might be appropriate at such events, apprising employees of the organization's financial performance and praising them for their efforts. It may also be an ideal opportunity to advise of changes in organizational status or extol employees to greater efforts in a certain direction.

As mentioned in chapter 2, the leader should, where possible, take time to personally induct new recruits, imparting in particular the organizational ethos and opportunity for personal growth. Again, this personal commitment by the most senior executive officer of the organization will leave an indelible impression on the new recruit and convince them of the importance of the organizational ethos from the beginning of their tenure.

The leader should personally, and individually, advise employees of their bonus and the outcome of their salary review. The basis of the awards should be discussed and ways to improve performance explored. The employee should leave this review in a positive, and motivated, frame of mind, irrespective of the outcome of the awards.

The leader should take an active role in defining and understanding the organization's product/service portfolio and in setting target markets. Not only will this ensure that the leader's experience and knowledge are passed on but ensures that the organization's output matches demand.

The leader should ensure that they are available to meet customers at any stage of a contact. This may be to assist in a sale or to help in resolving a dispute. In each case, the leader will be able to access the highest levels of the customer's organization when subordinates cannot. Such interventions should only be made in full consultation with those responsible for the day-to-day function and without appearing to undermine these employees in the eyes of their colleagues or customers.

Lose the Ego

HUMILITY IS THE WATCHWORD.

The leader must approach a task in a selfless manner that eschews the impression of ego. Humility is the watchword. Accordingly, organizational goals should not be self-centered. In other words, goals should be about what is good for the organization and the employees, not what is good for the leader or senior management. For example, it is not unknown for a leader, or senior management, to delay publishing results, or to hide problems, until after bonuses have been awarded. This is to ignore the collective good and must be avoided. In the long-term, it is counterproductive in any case.

Praise should be about extolling the virtues of employees, not the leader. If a leader is praised, or thanked by an employee, the leader should turn this around. For example, an employee thanks the leader for resolving a work problem. The leader should reply along the lines of, "You're welcome, but thank you for bringing it to my attention."

A leader should never talk in the first person when describing what the organization is doing or has achieved. It should always be "we" and never "I."

The wise leader intuitively understands that to have more talented people within their peer group does not diminish their own standing but works to the betterment of the organization. Indeed, the leader should ensure that they hire personnel who fill the gaps in their own knowledge and experience. Such a leader will laud and harness the talent around them and ensure that it is used constructively. Repressing talent to hide their own shortcomings is an anathema to the Empowerment Paradigm leader. The leader should ensure that this attitude permeates to lower levels of the organization. For example, project managers should view talent within their project teams as an advantage and use it to improve project outcomes rather than repress it to improve their own standing.

Interaction with Employees

When interacting with employees, a leader should use as a guide how they, themselves, would want to be treated. Nobody enjoys being ignored, bullied, or patronized.

Never criticize an employee, especially in the heat of the moment or in front of other employees. This induces fear in the employee and those witnessing it. If you call an employee an idiot, they will tend to feel that they are. Criticism must be constructive and result in the employee having a firm target to improve their performance.

> ABUSIVE LEADERS, WHO INDUCE FEAR AS A LEADERSHIP SKILL, HAVE FEW LOYAL FOLLOWERS.

Abusive leaders, who induce fear as a leadership skill, have few loyal followers and will reap the rewards when they are in need of the efforts and support of their employees and this is not forthcoming or is halfhearted.

A leader must seek to understand an employee's motivation when they agree and when asked, or volunteer, to perform an additional task. An employee may automatically agree to further work when they do not, in fact, have the time or capability to do so because they feel it is expected of them. A leader must ensure that employees understand that they are permitted to decline tasks in these circumstances, and indeed, it is encouraged that they tell the truth in this regard. When this happens, the leader should praise the employee for their candor, provided it is not perceived by the leader as shirking.

Transparency and Honesty

A leader should be transparent at all times. For example, if a leader informs employees that a project award is expected and this does not transpire, the leader should tell those same employees that the previous assertion was premature and explain why the project was not awarded.

If a leader treats an employee badly, then they must apologize. Transparency, honesty, and genuine humility in a leader set an example to all employees, which may deter the practice of hiding mistakes and improve resolution outcomes.

Motivational Targets

> THE CEO CAN PLAY A KEY ROLE IN PROVIDING INFORMAL MOTIVATIONAL TARGETS.

The leader can play a key role in providing informal motivational targets.

For example, a project manager may have achieved a record margin on a project. When a similar project arises, the leader might informally tell the same, or another, project manager that it would be good to break the record for the margin on the new project. This focuses the mind of the project manager, who can motivate their team to attain this goal. Should the target be achieved, this should be recognized when a bonus is awarded and mentioned specifically as a contributory factor.

Dispute Resolution and Project Closure

An area where leaders are clearly at an advantage to employees is in the resolution of customer disputes and the closure of projects.

Employees who are used to the leader taking a direct hand in day-to-day matters and who are comfortable and confident in their own roles will not hesitate to use the leader as a tool for resolving disputes with customers and closing projects.

It is not an exaggeration to state that the profit of a sale, job, or project exists largely in its successful closure. Customers often withhold payment, pending resolution of disputes or perceived inadequacy of supply. A customer may do so as a matter of course to the improvement of its own cash flow and to the detriment of suppliers. On the other hand, a customer may have a valid reason for withholding final payment or imposing a penalty.

Whatever the circumstances, employees should be encouraged to approach the leader to, firstly, advise of the impact on the organization and, secondly, to ask for assistance. This is an example of where the employee must feel comfortable in approaching the leader for help even when the sale, job, or project has gone wrong. The corollary is that the leader must praise the employee for bringing the matter to their attention and seek to resolve the matter in conjunction with that employee. Asking for assistance in this regard should not be perceived as a sign of weakness by the employee, their colleagues, or the leader.

Mistakes that have been made must be treated as described in chapter 2. In short, employees must know that they have the unequivocal support of the leader, irrespective of any mistakes made or where the responsibility for those mistakes lies.

> EMPLOYEES MUST KNOW THAT THEY HAVE THE UNEQUIVOCAL SUPPORT OF THE CEO.

Such leader level intervention may include assisting the employee to resolve the matter with their customer counterpart, the leader writing to a level above the customer counterpart's level, and arranging to meet with the customer.

In order not to undermine the employee seeking help in the eyes of their colleagues and customers, the leader shall ensure that the employee is kept informed about (and openly copied on correspondence) or directly involved with whatever action the leader deems is necessary.

Chapter Five

Natural Organizational Improvements (Realized through the Prism of the Empowerment Paradigm)

The Empowerment Paradigm Difference

As previously explored, many organizations languish in a climate of deliberating fear with departmental structures and excessive, and costly, layers of management, which interfere with intraorganizational communication and sustain unnecessary bureaucratic controls.

In contrast, the first four chapters have shown how replacing fear with trust within the workplace, building the individual and collective morale, and setting and committing to a purposeful and ethical identity, all enthusiastically and relentlessly driven through by an unwavering, compassionate leader allows an organization to attain the confidence to cast asides these burdens and free itself to exploit the latent potential of its employees and, in so doing, dramatically improve the operational efficiency, potential for growth, and optimism about the future. Chapter 6 describes how to recognize when the transformation is complete.

In this chapter, we shall consider how this new dynamic and confident working environment automatically steers the organization toward implementing major operational improvements. In essence, it will demonstrate that if the strictures of the Empowerment Paradigm are properly instituted and the complete Empowerment Paradigm organization attained, then improvements, and optimization, will automatically flow in many key operational areas. This self-adjustment is what separates the Empowerment Paradigm from other business philosophies. It is the Empowerment Paradigm Difference.

In order to illustrate this self-adjusting phenomenon, we shall examine in detail, making use of case studies, several significant areas of improvements. These can best be categorized as

ORGANIZATIONAL IMPROVEMENTS

FUNCTIONAL IMPROVEMENTS

QUALITATIVE IMPROVEMENTS

Each is examined in this chapter.

Organizational Improvements

Organizational Improvements

Organizational improvements realized in Empowerment Paradigm organizations relate to the way in which an organization is structured: its orientation, its operational complexity, its size, and its costs. Four aspects are considered in detail, namely as follows:

REFOCUSING OPERATIONAL ORIENTATION

Supporting the organization's most profitable activities

SIMPLIFICATION OF FUNCTION AND DOCUMENTATION

Eliminating duplication and reducing complexity and documentation

ESTABLISHING ORGANIZATIONAL SIZE

Finding the correct size and skills mixed with a degree of flexibility

REDUCING COSTS

Creating an unrelenting and self-determining downward pressure on costs

Refocusing Operational Orientation

Maximizing Flexibility and Profitability

The Empowerment Paradigm Difference dictates that an organization automatically seeks to support and improve its most profitable functions and so ensures that operations focus upon maximizing profitability.

As referred to in chapter 2, a natural benefit of utilizing the Empowerment Paradigm methodologies is to establish a clear, and understandable, direction of travel, which affords an organization the opportunity and the flexibility to assess and reorientate its focus, from time-to-time as required, in order to support its profit centers and maximize profit.

Nurturing and Releasing the Talent

The success of refocusing the operational function of an organization, and the creation of a talented workforce, depends upon that organization being able to properly harness methodology-enhanced employee traits, such as confidence, aspiration, motivation, transfer of skills, multifunctionality, increased responsibility, and accountability.

The Empowerment Paradigm organization not only allows existing employees' talent to flourish but also encourages employees to develop new skills and talents, which enhance the organizational skill-mix and talent-pool.

An organization that can properly utilize its employees' talent without a top-heavy, managerial-led hierarchy is able to create project-focused teams, which draw upon a pool of multifunctional talent and so optimizes operational efficiency.

A Focus on Contracts

Departmental organizations inherently operate as blunt tools, which invariably serve the structure of an organization, rather than its profit centers. The Empowerment Paradigm Difference allows organizations to dispense with functional departments and associated department managers. This automatically results in a reduction in layers of management and so sharpens the organization focus upon optimizing contract execution and maximizing profitability.

This project-focused approach with power and accountability residing in the hands of a team leader or project manager is far more effective than departmental structures where departmental managers are focused upon, and responsible for, nothing more than the performance of their function.

Empowering Project Managers

In contract-focused organizations, the project manager is the linchpin. Project managers will be ambitious, multiskilled employees who are given sole responsibility and accountability for a contract. The Empowerment Paradigm Difference ensures such project managers are identified, trained, and afforded the opportunity to flourish.

To the customer, after the contract is awarded, the project manager *is* the organization. This extends the importance of good project management far beyond the actual function. Good project managers will promote and maintain good relations with customers and individuals within the customer's organization. The project manager is the central point of contact between an organization and its customer.

How project managers conduct themselves is, therefore, not only a matter of operational efficiency but also one of probity, deportment, and personal chemistry. To all extents and purposes, project managers are conducting one-to-one public relations every time they have contact with a customer and individuals within the customer's organization. The Empowerment Paradigm Difference ensures that an organization fully supports its project managers in this vital role and exploits it to the best advantage.

Case Study

Company A designs, supplies, and installs pressure vessels to various industry sectors. Traditionally, Company A would expect its sales team to negotiate contract change orders at the end of a project. This often involves the sales team members approaching customers for the first time since the order was placed. This disconnect does not exploit the relationship established between the project manager and the customer during project execution.

The Empowerment Paradigm Difference automatically recognizes the importance of the project manager-customer relationship and authorizes the project manager to issue and negotiate contract change orders during the execution of the project. Empowered project managers with responsibility for the bottom line are best placed to achieve the most favorable fiscal outcome.

By their efforts, project managers may also help to ensure that customers give preference, or even sole supplier status, to an organization and so help in securing new and repeat orders.

Project managers, overseeing all project functions, will directly identify or be informed of problems arising or mistakes made without having the hierarchical impediment of departmental management. The same principle applies to intraproject team communication where project team members working closely together benefit from a lateral flow of information and so become immediately aware of issues without departmental barriers.

The Role of the Project Team

In the Empowerment Paradigm organization, freed from the constraint of departmental structures, project managers can draw into their team multifunctional employees who cover several project disciplines. Project managers will ensure that each project team is functionally complete. Project managers tasked with more than one contract are able to use project experiences and effective innovations to the benefit of new projects. In short, project managers controlling multidisciplinary teams will have a complete view of all project activities, which significantly improves operational efficiency and, in particular, enables swift and effective corrective action to mitigate problems arising. Project managers will, as a matter of course, communicate their experiences freely with other project managers, ensuring that corrective actions are made in all applicable circumstances and do not become lost or isolated within rigid departmental structures.

Project team members may also be tasked with working on more than one project. Such porous project team boundaries and overlap of project personnel substantially improve the flow of knowledge and experience throughout the Empowerment Paradigm organization and, again, automatically reduce the dangers inherent in losing valuable information derived from each project. Once again, this also ensures that innovations or solutions to problems, which occur during project execution, never occur in isolation and so become available to other project teams.

Case Study

Company A comprises various project teams, each assigned a contract. Project managers and project team members are multifunctional and interact with and assist other project teams.

The Empowerment Paradigm Difference dictates that Company A will have no departmental structures and functional responsibility, and accountability will be devolved to the project level. Consequently, project team members freely exchange information with other project teams.

On one project, a design error on a vessel support structureresulted in costly on-site modifications. Project team members, empowered to pass on this information directly to other project teams without the constraints of department hierarchies, automatically ensure that this error is not replicated.

The multifunctionality of project team members that is automatically conferred by the Empowerment Paradigm Difference has several direct and indirect benefits when an organization is project-orientated. It reduces the number of disciplinary interfaces and so improves intraproject team communication, as well as enhances operational and technical integration. It prevents inherent disciplinary interface difficulties from becoming lost or ignored. It increases the scope for creativity and innovation, which can lead to product and process improvements.

Driving through the Philosophy

As explored in chapter 3, organizational mantras are a valuable tool, which bind project teams in a unity of purpose and enable project managers to improve project performance. For example, a simple mantra such as "Getting the goods to site fast" may provide the impetuous and focus to ensure an organization can offer industry-best lead times in delivering goods to the customer.

Case Study

Company A extols, as a virtue, its short projects' lead times.

Because of the Empowerment Paradigm Difference, Company A is so confident that it can beat all competition in the shortest delivery time to a job site that it invites customers to penalize it for late delivery and offer a bonus for early delivery. Customers find this attractive as delayed project schedules are always a problem.

In this way, Company A is incentivized to substantially improve project lead times, allowing the customer to complete its engineering, planning, requisitioning and placement of purchase orders earlier. The customer is then able to mobilize site activities ahead of schedule. Company A's short project lead time demonstrates its efficiency and improves its reputation, resulting in additional orders and an enhanced bottom line.

Such a mantra assists not only in focusing team efforts but provides, as consequence, a powerful marketing tool. The Empowerment Paradigm Difference ensures an organization to automatically understand the advantage this confers and allows absolute freedom to exploit this to their best advantage.

Increased Accountability and Responsibility

In accordance with the Empowerment Paradigm principles, experienced project managers with a proven track record of success enjoy the confidence of senior management and are encouraged to execute a project in their own way. This trust invariably evokes a response from project managers to do all within their power to improve their project performance and not to disappoint. The corollary to such trust by management is that all project team members know that they will be recognized for any additional effort and improved performance.

Case Study

A project manager in Company A becomes aware that an executive wishes to place a purchase order with a steel vendor. The project manager knows that the performance of that steel vendor is questionable and may affect the project costs and impact upon the project margin. The project manager sees little value to the project in working with that steel vendor and is aware of his direct accountability for the project margin.

The Empowerment Paradigm Difference affords the project manager the authority to object to placing the steel order with this vendor and asks the CEO to ensure that no such order is placed. This subordinate intervention is welcomed and fully understood by senior management within the Empowerment Paradigm organization where profit margins are incentivized by rewarding attainment at all levels.

Increasing project managerial accountability in this way drives up operational standards through enhanced quality and fewer errors, shortens project schedules, and drives down costs and so increases the bottom line. This automatic benefit of employing the Empowerment Paradigm principles transfers organizational power to the project level and is a powerful tool in enhancing project margins.

Recognition and Reward

As described above, the Empowerment Paradigm Difference enables an organization to focus upon the needs of the project and supports project managers in their role as organizational figurehead while making them responsible and accountable for the success or, otherwise, of that role. It further ensures that project managers and all project team members know, and trust, they will be recognized and rewarded for improving project performance, increasing customer satisfaction and enhancing project margins.

Refocusing the Sales Function

The Empowerment Paradigm Difference automatically ensures that sales managers and sales teams, which handle prospective contracts up until award and formal handover to the assigned project manager, operate in a similar vein to project managers and project team members—that is, orientated toward the prospective contract, putting together multidisciplinary teams comprising multifunctional sales team members. Again, management ensures that sales managers are both responsible and accountable and understand the need to limit costs and so lower overheads, which increases the bottom line and the rewards on offer to the sales team.

In the Empowerment Paradigm organization, a sales team will naturally assess the effectiveness of the sales strategy and focus its energies upon products/services that have a high proposal-to-success rate. Invariably, it is these products and services that attract the lowest sales—and proposals-related costs. However, the Empowerment Paradigm organization will constantly strive to find ways to improve other less profitable products/services in order to make them more attractive to the market and so more profitable rather than waste resources upon out-of-date or superseded product/service lines or products/services.

The Empowerment Paradigm Difference ensures sales teams instinctively understand it is their responsibility to provide continuous feedback as to the competitiveness of organizational product and to find ways to improve product efficiency, competiveness, and so profitability. This will include providing information and ideas on how to meet new market demands and regulatory requirements.

The Empowerment Paradigm project and sales managers will also ensure their activities overlap to the extent that information, and knowledge, acquired by their respective functions is made freely available at handover meetings and other forums for functional interface.

Simplification of Function and Documentation

Shake Off Complicated Ways of Working

The Empowerment Paradigm Difference dictates that an organization constantly strives to simplify its function and documentation in order to increase operational efficiency, reduce costs, and maximize profitability.

The simplification of function and documentation flows naturally in organizations that utilize the Empowerment Paradigm methodology. Organizations adopting these principles automatically see their operations shake off unnecessarily complicated and bureaucratically ensnared ways of working and become leaner and more effective as a consequence.

A Clear Direction of Travel

As described in chapter 3, senior management will have set a direction of travel for an organization through its vision, mission, and values.

As a direct result, an organization will have evaluated and distilled its operational output. This evaluation comprises four stages and will occur naturally in organizations that fully adopt the principles embodied within the Empowerment Paradigm.

Firstly, the organization, from time to time, assesses and defines for each of its products/services the territory, the total market size, the available market, and the target market share. This evaluation process will include identifying new markets for existing, improved, or new products/services.

Secondly and concurrently, the organization thoroughly assesses each one of its products/services against its potential in the identified available and new markets. The range of products/services offered is adjusted accordingly and required improvements identified.

Thirdly, the organization assesses its future target markets trends, identifying the need for improved products/services required to meet new regulations, and improved supply from competitors, or alternatively, develop new products/services to meet these requirements.

Finally, the organization assesses its staffing, ensuring the correct level of manpower and skills mix to match the organizational objectives and to meet this assessment. This includes ensuring sufficient sales and proposals team members, possessing the talent and product knowledge to match sales targets, and ensuring sufficient engineers with correct skills mix and product knowledge to execute their function and creative skills to improve existing and develop new products/services.

The Empowerment Paradigm employees have the drive to match organizational aspiration, tempered by a realism of what can feasibly be achieved and born of the confidence conferred by the methodology.

Clarity of organizational purpose in these respects enables organizational function to focus and simplify. Functional objectives will productively, and accurately, channel the increased levels of confidence, creativity, and innovation naturally released by the Empowerment Paradigm.

Encouraging Talent

As explored in chapter 2, the Empowerment Paradigm organization values, nurtures, and rewards its employees and, in particular, the most knowledgeable, talented, and innovative ones. These employees possess the ability to constantly improve existing products/services and invent new ones in order to maintain, or attain, technological advantage and meet changing market conditions and requirements. Such employees are the engine of creativity, which allows the organization the flexibility to maintain and enhance its market position and reach into new markets. As is often the case, with creativity comes idiosyncratic behavior.

The Empowerment Paradigm organization instinctively knows how to manage such behavior and harness this talent to the best effect. Taking the time and making the effort to understand and accommodate the behavior of its original thinkers is a guaranteed way for an organization to generate the new ideas that can lead to market advantage.

Using Reliable Suppliers to Maximum Advantage

The Empowerment Paradigm organization intuitively understands that to accurately replicate the function, time after time and without error, reduces project lead times, reduces costs, enhances quality, improves profitability, and satisfies customers. Accordingly, the Empowerment Paradigm Difference ensures that time and effort is taken to develop relationships with reliable suppliers who are able to supply goods and services of the highest quality and can meet the tightest of schedules.

By maximizing each supplier's scope, the Empowerment Paradigm organization is able to minimize the number of suppliers and so further reduce project execution costs and the number of supplier-to-supplier interfaces. This principle extends to asking suppliers to trail fit their supply in their works to ensure fit on site, simplification of function, and reducing expensive-to-remedy on-site nonconformities, which lead to reduced project costs.

Supplier relationships can, in some cases, develop into formal partnerships and, in exceptional circumstances, into single-source supply where a common product/component is required for many contracts and the security of reliable delivery and quality at an agreed competitive price simplifies both function and documentation. Single-source supply relationships also simplify other organizational functions, such as technical and commercial evaluation and quality control and expediting, as well as substantially reducing project execution costs.

Case Study

Company B designs, engineers, and supplies structural steelwork to various industry sectors. It subcontracts the fabrication of the steelwork.

Company B's procurement policy stipulates that at least three competitive bids are required before placing the order for the structural steelwork. This will require inquiries to be sent to more than three suppliers (as some may not be able, or willing, to bid). Each bid requires a technical evaluation and bid tab evaluation for price. Company B will also have to thoroughly check all shop floor drawings from the selected supplier for accuracy and interface, as well as ensuring that delivery requirements are understood and met. New suppliers are also required to undergo a quality audit in order to attain approved supplier status.

The Empowerment Paradigm Difference dictates that Company B will strive where a realistic opportunity exists to form a sole supplier partnership with a reliable, high quality steel supplier. This allows Company B to dispense with a substantial amount of the technical, commercial, and bureaucratic procedures set out above. For example, Company B knows its trusted sole supplier can commence drafting shop floor drawings on the first issue of technical documentation and specifications rather than engage in a technical evaluation and a query-response dialogue. This reduces both engineering man-hours for both parties and improves project lead times immeasurably. The intimate working relationship between the sole supplier and Company B means that the division in the engineering function is properly delineated and duplication of work is avoided, leading to reduced costs and schedules. The sole supplier understands Company B's supply and markets and so is able to concentrate on supply interfaces where nonconformities tend to arise. This advance knowledge reduces engineering review man-hours and dramatically reduces site-related remedial work and consequent back charges and schedule delay penalties.

In these ways, Company B is able to simplify both its function and documentation. This allows Company B to offer significantly shorter supply lead times than its competitors, as well as to reduce cost and improve both competitiveness and margins.

The Empowerment Paradigm Difference also automatically ensures that suppliers deliver to suit the organization's requirements and not their own. For example, a steel supplier may fabricate all members of a certain size at one time. This is cost-effective in pure manufacturing terms. However, the organization may require only a limited number of these, plus several other sizes, on-site to meet construction requirements at any one time. In these circumstances, the supplier knows that it must deliver only what is required to the job site. Using the same example, the Empowerment Paradigm organization also understands the advantages of developing a piece-marking method, which enables site operatives to receive, store, and erect materials so as to optimize the construction function.

Reliable partnerships with trusted suppliers may also be used to simplify the function and documentation by eliminating some of the organization's work that is duplicated by the vendor.

The Empowerment Paradigm Difference ensures that allowing the vendor to maintain and control the documents relating to its supply, eliminates a substantial amount of duplication and reduces the number of documents to a more manageable level. This simplification of function and documentation makes it possible to ensure that all documents are current and amendments are universally applied. Substantial less documents makes the document amendment process less complex, less burdensome and avoids the potential for costly errors and nonconformities.

Case Study

Company B assesses its engineering documentation and realizes that it has up to five hundred drawings for each type of steel structure it supplies. Engineering detail that is contained in Company B's own drawings is duplicated on many of its vendor's shop floor drawings. For this reason, the drawing amendment process has become unnecessarily complex and burdensome with the details on some of Company B's drawings remaining unchanged throughout a project and failing to reflect the changes made on the vendor shop floor drawings.

The Empowerment Paradigm difference ensures that Company B automatically strives to reduce the number of its engineering drawings to a more manageable level (in this case, an average of fifty per product) primarily as a result of allowing the vendor to maintain and control the product drawings relating to its shop floor supply, thus eliminating a substantial amount of duplication of drawings. This simplification of function and documentation further helps to ensure that all drawings are accurate and amendments are universally applied, thus avoiding the potential for costly errors and nonconformities during project execution.

The Role of Project and Sales Managers

Project and sales managers, responsible and accountable for costs, ensure that all functions within their teams are performed as simply and cost effectively as possible. Self-confident individual team members, encouraged and empowered to innovate and improve their own and others' function, fully understand and trust that any improvements made will be recognized and rewarded. This automatic drive to simplify function is the Empowerment Paradigm Difference.

Quality of Supply Reduces Documentation

Simplification of organizational documentation flows naturally from the goal of simplification of function. For example, reducing the number of design changes reduces the number of document revisions per project. Improved levels of quality and targets to minimize the number of nonconformities will assist in this respect. The Empowerment Paradigm organization automatically understands this and uses its quality management system as a simplification tool.

Establishing Organizational Size

The Fear of Change

Establishing the size of an organization is always fraught with difficulty. Decreasing the size of the workforce is potentially one of the most disruptive and morale-destroying processes an organization can undertake.

Even increasing the size of the workforce brings with it the added complications. Chapter 2 looks at how job insecurity is a significant cause of fear within the workplace. However, the loss of individual purpose and direction in an enlarged or too large organization has its own problems. Increasing the workforce without maintaining the organizational focus on meeting its clearly defined objectives can lead to a dilution, or reversal, of the Empowerment Paradigm principles. In such circumstances, project teams can become too large, lines of communication become blocked or are severed, and general malaise can infect the individual and collective morale. Employees become detached, feel cast adrift, and feelings of anxiety and insecurity inevitably ensue.

Fear-Free Change

The key to ensuring a smooth transition in organization size is the Empowerment Paradigm Difference whereby the organization intuitively understands how to reconcile the positions of creating, or maintaining, a fear-free working environment while establishing the correct size of an organization. That is, every action the organization takes is based upon the need for stability and security as envisaged through the prism of the Empowerment Paradigm methodology.

Built-in Trends

As previously illustrated, the Empowerment Paradigm organization will have within it mechanisms that automatically direct it to the correct size and skill-mix. For example, project managers with responsibility and accountability for the bottom line will not tolerate excessive levels of staffing nor will they allow a project to be detrimentally affected by understaffing or the incorrect mix of skills. Senior management, therefore, takes note of project managers when determining the correct size of the organization. Changes in workload will preferably be met by a mixture of maximizing the use of existing project team resources and outsourcing certain activities managed by an empowered project manager.

Case Study

Company C is growing, its turnover increasing by 50 percent in a single year and the prospects for further growth in the future.

The Empowerment Paradigm Difference dictates that senior management in Company C listens to its project managers with respect to present capabilities and meets the increase in demand by a mixture of maximizing the use of existing project team resources and outsourcing certain activities rather than simply hiring new staff to expand the project teams. By keeping control of gross and net overheads in this way, in times of high demand, Company C ensures that it is best placed to weather any downturn in demand in the longer term. Not only does this policy ensure commensurately reduced variations in overheads in response to greater fluctuations in demand, but it reduces the disruption and impact on morale associated with constantly changing levels of staffing.

The Empowerment Paradigm organization will have set clear objectives and direction of travel through its vision, mission, and values. As a direct result, the organization will have evaluated and distilled its operational output in terms of product/service portfolio and have set goals to improve and expand this.

The tangible benefits of the Empowerment Paradigm methodology automatically confers upon an organization to optimize its size are manifold. As discussed elsewhere in this chapter, these include a natural tendency to reduce layers of management by focusing on the project, simplifying function, lessening bureaucracy, the transfer of knowledge and skills within the organization, and increased multifunctionality of employees. All of these benefits, inherent within the Empowerment Paradigm organization, afford senior management the opportunity to understand the optimal size of the organization and bring about stability.

Rightsizing

As discussed later in this chapter, each employee carries both an overhead and unit cost to a varying extent. As such, rightsizing an organization to properly meet its objective is critical to its commercial success and depends upon the existing mix and level of the skills within the work force and that available on the jobs market. For example, multiskilled employees might have more value to the organization than monoskilled. However, a highly monoskilled employee might be of more value to the organization than a lower multiskilled employee.

The Empowerment Paradigm Difference dictates that the value of monoskilled, multiskilled and long-serving employees is recognized and ensures that these employees are eager to transfer their knowledge to younger and less experienced members of the organization. In this way, valuable knowledge is not lost and the younger and less experienced employees are properly educated and trained to adequately support the execution of the selected product/services portfolio in the targeted, available market.

Case Study

Company C employs several designers. Mostly, these designers are capable of turning their hand to the design and engineering processes of all company products. However, one long-serving designer can really only effectively design the Company C's oldest core product. This designer has an in-depth knowledge of this product that is unparalleled within Company C.

The Empowerment Paradigm Difference ensures that Company C recognizes the value of the long-serving designer and ensures that this key employee is eager to transfer his knowledge so that the other designers learn all they can regarding the core product. In this way, valuable knowledge is not lost to Company C, and the younger designers learn that their own knowledge will receive equal veneration in the future.

In order to accord with the requirements of the market, senior management within the Empowerment Paradigm organization undertake, from time to time, a thorough review of the size and skills mix required when reassessing the organization's available markets, product/service portfolio, and organizational aspiration. The size and skills mix must enable the organization to properly support the targeted, available market and to service the forecast sales volume and the execution of the selected product/services portfolio. This process, implemented transparently and with employee input, serves as baseline for optimizing the size of the organization (see Simplification of Function and Documentation).

Outsourcing

Part of the rightsizing process requires senior management to make a periodic assessment of future demand. This requires constant reappraisal, but there are ways to mitigate the fluctuations in demand that requires senior management to fully understand the level and mix of skills within the organization. For example, part of the rightsizing process may be to outsource certain activities, let us say, the drafting function in an engineering company. However, the organization maintains the capability to produce drawings internally when rightsizing the organization. A minimum number of engineers with drafting skills are retained in order to service a baseline workload and are explicitly advised by the organization that these skills are still of value. This affords the organization some degree of flexibility when demand falls and some, or all, of the drafting function can be brought back in-house. This will also require the organization to have contractual flexibility with its outsourced vendors. As noted in chapter 2, this has the added benefit of increasing job security during lulls between projects or general economic downturns.

As employees claim that they can perform the outsourced work themselves for fear of losing their jobs management must ensure those employees that their jobs are not under threat. This must be clearly explained in order to avoid confusion and to maintain stability. This is something that the organization will intuitively understand and is the Empowerment Paradigm Difference.

Case Study

Company C has made a strategic decision to outsource a significant proportion of its drafting function.

The Empowerment Paradigm Difference dictates that Company C takes time to ensure that the decision to outsource is properly explained to its employees. During discussions, these employees claim that they can perform the outsourced work themselves for fear of losing their jobs. Company C's management ensures that the employees are reassured that their jobs are not under threat and made to understand that outsourcing is beneficial to the organization and employees as it facilitates stability and job security for employees by smoothing out organizational workloads as demand fluctuates.

However, Company C also ensures that its employees are trained to manage the activities of the outsourced company. This gives employees new skills, improves oversight and interface with the outsourced company, and keeps them involved in day-to-day matters that will assist them should the outsourcing policy be reversed if demand falls. It further enhances morale for employees to take on supervisory tasks.

By taking these measures, the Empowerment Paradigm organization has set a clear direction of travel with assessment of its future manpower requirements and skills mix. It will also have fully exploited outsourcing as a strategic policy to cope with fluctuating levels of demand and thereby minimizing the disruption caused by the cyclical need to adjust staffing levels, improving employees' job security and instilling a sense of optimism about their future.

Assessing the correct size of an organization is something that the Empowerment Paradigm organization does on a regular basis, both automatically by its built-in processes and also on a deliberate, objective basis.

Optimizing Skills Mix

Senior management ensures that the organizational size and mix of skills matches organizational objectives. From time to time, each employee will be assessed against these criteria. Fully appreciating the merits, faults, and idiosyncrasies of employees is critical to this assessment, and the sometimes incongruous characteristics displayed by employees are not always easy to understand or reconcile with the organizational good. For example, a particular employee may appear high maintenance, constantly requiring attention and management time. But that same employee may be a brilliant innovator whose ideas have improved product design and increased sales. This employee should be retained and nurtured despite the downside to their behavior.

This employee assessment process is performed, when the need arises, discreetly without alerting, or alarming, the organization. This is where the virtues of the Empowerment Paradigm methodology are vital. Senior management will, as described in chapter 3, have immersed themselves in the day-to-day operation of the organization. They will already know much about each employee, professionally and personally. In such circumstances, any additional inquiries, correction, or praise will not seem starkly out of place or raise suspicion or cause fear.

In the Empowerment Paradigm organization, senior management instinctively uses this as an opportunity to reiterate to employees the organizational strategy in terms of future job security, what attributes the organization values in employees, how the employee can contribute, the opportunities that exist for career growth, and the rewards that are on offer.

The Empowerment Paradigm organization also understands that training employees with innate and valuable skills to meet exact organizational requirements is a useful way of optimizing operational efficiency without needing to adjust its size. As the Empowerment Paradigm employees are keen to attain different or better skills and to take on greater responsibility, they are receptive to any training that is offered. This is particularly useful when new products/services are introduced. Senior management will understand the existing skills mix and so will be better able to determine if these are able to meet the new product/service requirements or if new skills are required via training of existing employees or bringing in new staff. Congruously, the Empowerment Paradigm employee will be incentivized and motivated to take on new tasks and training required to fulfill this task.

It imparts confidence and stability when employees see that senior management are intimately involved in keeping the organization both rightsized and on the right track and, as such, are more trusted and respected when they are seen to get their hands dirty when difficult and sensitive matters arise. These increased trust and respect help management deal with these issues more quickly and effectively. The Employment Paradigm Difference ensures senior management understands this and, therefore, not adverse to immersing themselves in difficult and delicate situations.

Reassuring Employees

In the rightsized organization, senior management must ensure that the principles of the Empowerment Paradigm methodology are rigorously reinforced. This takes the form of a sustained effort on the part of senior management to personally assure employees of their role within and value to the organization and to help in resolving difficulties, which will inevitably arise as those employees adjust to any changes to their present, new, or additional duties and responsibilities. A common fear or complaint from employees in these circumstances is that they might not be able to cope with their new role or increased responsibilities. Such employees need to have the trust of and be supported by senior management, who show confidence in their abilities, and to be reassured that they are trusted and capable. If senior management assesses employees thoroughly prior to the rightsizing process, such faith will not be unfounded or go unrewarded. The Empowerment Paradigm Difference ensures that senior management are automatically steered to this supportive kind of behavior.

The Rightsized Organization

The final position of a rightsized organization should be one that is stable, dynamic, flexible, self-assured, possessing the right mix and level of skills, multifunctional, cohesive, and most importantly, successful. In short, this is an Empowerment Paradigm organization.

Reducing Costs

Room For Greater Rewards

Bearing down upon the costs is a relentless and necessary task in nearly all organizations.

This struggle, when viewed through the prism of the Empowerment Paradigm methodology, becomes less prescriptive, less divisive, and so considerably more effective. Instilling the virtues of reducing the level of costs, as part of this methodology, results in a self-determining, self-perpetuating, bottom-up approach where cost savings do not just go to the bottom line but also make room for greater rewards for all employees. This is the Empowerment Paradigm Difference.

Proportionality

A fundamental precept for organizations embarking upon cost-saving programs is not to cut so aggressively as to make false economies. Sacrificing quality on the altar of economy is something that should be anathema to all organizations. The recent travails of companies within the automotive sector are a warning to all organizations in this respect.

Instilling the Message on Controlling Costs

Once employees trust and understand that all cost saving programs are administered equally and fairly throughout an organization, senior management will be in a position to implement surprisingly ambitious schemes, which substantially reduce costs. This imbued culture encourages and incentivizes employees to drive through the cost savings and make suggestions for even greater savings. The Empowerment Paradigm methodologies, as described in earlier chapters, ensure that employees understand the egalitarian nature of a cost reduction program and are fully empowered to fully engage in such a program enthusiastically, confidentially, and innovatively.

The Empowerment Paradigm Difference ensures that cost reduction is not seen by the organization as burdensome but as an opportunity to further grow the business and to increase the profitability of the Company. Employees also know and trust that some of the cost savings will be passed to them as a performance bonus.

Case Study

Company D is a small engineering company that is determined to drive down its costs. It embarks upon a series of cost-saving measures, including more stringent control of travel expenses, stationery supplies, and timekeeping.

The Empowerment Paradigm Difference ensures that Company D's employees fully embrace these measures because they know and trust that they apply to all employees including the CEO and that some of the savings will be passed to them as a performance bonus.

The natural benefits automatically derived from the Empowerment Paradigm methodology in terms of reducing costs include rightsizing through removing redundant levels of management and increased multifunctionality, a simplification of function that increases productivity and so reduces unit costs, improved product portfolio and technologies, improved quality of supply, fewer nonconformities and corrective actions, improved industrial relations, and reduced staff turnover.

As has been expounded previously, the propagation of instructional mantras, which focus on operational objectives, is vital in reducing costs. The basic edict to perform a task correctly at the first attempt when indoctrinated on an organizational basis has significant capacity to reduce costs. The bottom-up, self-determining, accountable, self-perpetuating principles enshrined within the Empowerment Paradigm release the power of mantras to improve operational efficiency and reduce costs.

Case Study

Company D operates by the simple mantra "Do it right first time" when designing and engineering its products. As part of this process, an engineer produces a data sheet, which is sent to a draftsman who, from the data contained therein, produces several engineering drawings. However, the data sheet contains a single error, which is incorporated into the said drawings. If the error had been identified by the process engineer prior to the issue, it would have been easily and cheaply corrected. If it is discovered after drawings have been made and issued, corrective actions are more time-consuming and costly.

The Empowerment Paradigm Difference ensures that Company D, by truly buying into and living by its mantra to "Do it right first time," avoids these unnecessary costs and delay in schedule resulting from propagating errors of this kind.

Payroll Costs

Most organizations understand that by far the largest proportion of overhead is payroll costs. The Empowerment Paradigm organization—with its project-focused structure, simplified function, and reduced layers of management—naturally requires fewer employees resulting in a lower level of overheads while simultaneously increasing operational focus, efficiency, and so productivity.

Managers and department heads carry a greater proportion of overhead cost than subordinate employees whose cost are more largely attributable to organizational output. The Empowerment Paradigm organization naturally dispenses with departmental structures and department heads and puts power in the hands of project managers. This realigns the management function to organizational output and so transfers overhead cost to the naturally more productive unit costs.

As referred to above, a key factor in reducing payroll costs the Empowerment Paradigm way is egalitarianism. In other words, cost savings are seen to apply equally to all levels of the organization. For example, it might be decided that company cars are a luxury an organization cannot afford. If such a policy is adopted, it is imperative that the CEO also turns up to work each morning in his own car. Fleets of company cars are never a good sign for customers visiting an organization. It speaks of excess and complacency when dynamism and quality of service is the image that needs to be projected. As in most jurisdictions, company cars confer little or no fiscal benefit to employees. Because of punitive taxation, company-supplied cars are no longer a perk. As such, using company cars in order to lure targeted employees to an organization is ultimately counterproductive and creates confusion and resentment in other employees.

The Empowerment Paradigm Difference ensures that the Company policy on employee benefits is accepted and propagated throughout the organization. Contracts with existing employees and new employees will only include performance related bonuses which ensures that all employees are incentivized towards maximazing profitability.

Case Study

Company D needs a new financial director. Recruitment agencies inform the head of HR in Company D that a competitive package must include an executive-type company car.

The Empowerment Paradigm Difference dictates that if accepted this will break the company policy on employee benefits. The CEO (even he does not have a company car) therefore instructs the recruiter to state in advertisements performance-related bonuses only apply. He then relies upon his own negotiating skills to entice his chosen candidate by offering performance bonuses that do not break the company policy. This avoids the resentment of existing staff at Company D and ensures that the financial director is incentivized toward maximizing profitability.

In a similar vein, senior management who want to connect with employees and be seen to be part of an organizational team will not have high-end perks, such as club membership, as part of their employment package. In eschewing the trappings of the position, senior management present a powerful message to all employees that will ensure that cost control programs are received more favorably, more effectively pursued, and cause the minimum of dissent. The last thing the Empowerment Paradigm CEO wants to hear is a sentence that starts, "Why shouldn't I have . . ." and continues "When he has . . ." Nothing is more certain to increase discontent and create barriers within an organization than sentiments of this kind, born of sense of hypocrisy and inequality.

By eliminating ineffective, and unfair, employment perks, the Empowerment Paradigm organization is automatically freed from the deadweight cost of unnecessary, nonperformance-related perks.

The Empowerment Paradigm Difference dictates that all types of benefits that cannot be applied at all levels of the organization are inappropriate and, ultimately, self-defeating.

Controlling Travel Costs

As most organizations require employees to travel on business to some extent or another in the Empowerment Paradigm organization, senior management ensures that the organization's business travel policy is carefully formulated on a cost-effective and egalitarian basis. It is vital that all employees understand and trust that this policy applies to all within the organization without exception.

It is then the project and sales managers who police the policy. They are incentivized to minimize travel costs by being accountable for the bottom line of the project and sales function. Accordingly, sales and project managers will assess the need to travel, the number of people traveling, the class of travel, grade of accommodation utilized, sustenance, and entertainment of clients.

The key is to ensure that all employees who travel, at whatever level, understand that reducing travel costs will benefit them personally. In other words, employees should ask themselves, Do I want to give some of my bonus away to an airline or hotel chain? The Empowerment

Paradigm Difference ensures that the instinctive answer to this question is an emphatic *no*.

Controlling Sales-Related Costs

A significant part of organizational overhead is directly attributable to the sales-and-proposals function. These costs are only transferred to a project when a contract is awarded and remain as overhead for unsuccessful bids. The Empowerment Paradigm organization will naturally manage these costs by monitoring the proposal-to-success rate and reducing the costs of the sales-and-proposals function by creating sales teams with multifunctional team members. Sales managers lead these teams and are made responsible and accountable for the cost of pursuing a contract.

Monitoring the proposal-to-success rate and how this relates to each product/service is vital to ensuring that sales and proposal costs are controlled and proportional. Stronger products/service will not only have a higher proposal-to-success rate but will also be easier and less costly to sell. For weaker products/services, the reverse is true. The empowered and accountable sales manager, operating within the Empowerment Paradigm organization, is automatically incentivized to minimize the sales-and-proposals function costs and optimize sales with acceptable levels of profit. In this way, the sales of the organization's stronger products/services are maximized. Accordingly, product/service portfolio selection, as described earlier in this chapter, is vital to controlling costs. Pursuing contracts for the sake of a sale, at any cost, or for individual and organizational prestige, is an anathema to the Empowerment Paradigm organization.

However, the Empowerment Paradigm organization will naturally strive to improve, where possible, those products/services and technologies that are demanded by the market but are not producing acceptable margins, as well as developing new products/services to meet that same demand.

Recognition and Reward

In the Empowerment Paradigm organization, all employees know and trust that savings that are made are both recognized and rewarded. In this way, employees, by their own actions, create room for the organization to increase the level of remuneration and bonus. This bottom-up, self-determining drive to improve organizational performance in return for reward is the engine that powers and self-perpetuates the Empowerment Paradigm. Project managers are encouraged to pursue enhanced profitability with determination and with a zeal that borders on the religious. A sacred bottom line has a powerful motivational impact upon the desire to reduce costs.

Fairness extends to the salary and bonus-award culture. The Empowerment Paradigm organization makes these awards proportionately. The CEO, or other senior manager, does not automatically merit proportionately larger bonuses than anyone else within the organization. Extraordinary performance can be rewarded by special bonuses. The reward process is transparent so as to prevent resentment and jealousy and to also serve as an incentive.

Case Study

Company D has had an extraordinary year financially. It has outperformed all its rivals and increased its profit margins when the general economy has been in downturn.

The sales and project teams have performed exceptionally well.

The CEO decides to announce an extraordinary midyear bonus.

The Empowerment Paradigm Difference dictates to reward all employees with the same bonus of 5 percent of the gross salary. The CEO further announces that if targets are met, the midyear bonus will be paid annually. This egalitarian policy confers a sense of organizational cohesion, which ensures all employees strive to meet the targets to trigger next year's midyear bonus.

Bonuses are also used as a powerful incentive to drive down unit costs. If an organization instills in all its employees, from the CEO down, the understanding that savings that are made will be transferred, if only in part, to the bonus levels, then the organization is institutionally incentivized to examine and bear down upon all kinds and levels of expenditure. The Empowerment Paradigm Difference automatically ensures this cooperative mindset is accepted and propagated throughout the organization.

Functional Improvements

Functional Improvements

Functional improvements realized in Empowerment Paradigm organizations relate to the way in which an organization operates procedurally in terms of the quality of its output, the welfare of its employees and others the organization interacts with, its environmental impact and image, and selling its output. Four functional aspects are considered in detail:

QUALITY

A bespoke quality management system designed to eliminate costly errors

HEALTH AND SAFETY

A focus on employee welfare, safe working practices, and management of incidents which ensure bid eligibility

ENVIRONMENT

A coherent and practical regime designed to mitigate operational impact on the environment and promote corporate image

SALES AND PROPOSALS

An incentivized, self-correcting function fully supported by and integrated within the wider organization

Quality

An Exemplary Level of Quality

The Empowerment Paradigm organization automatically strives, on an unrelenting basis, to provide an exemplary level of quality in the supply of its goods and services, and in contrast to other organizations, has built-in mechanisms that ensure that this is achieved and measured. This is the Empowerment Paradigm Difference.

Setting the Organizational Ethos

The vision, mission, and values set the framework for the organization's ethos on quality. Commitment to, and thorough propagation of quality-based mantras guide employees in attaining the required levels of quality and enshrine the organizational objective of minimizing nonconformities and expensive corrective actions.

In the Empowerment Paradigm organization, simple edicts, such as "Quality from the start" and "Do it right first time," imbue an employee's every action with direction and purpose.

Case Study

Company E provides outsourced drafting services to the various engineering companies.

The Empowerment Paradigm Difference means that Company E fully understands that introducing an error that is undetected at the design/engineering stage exacerbates problems as engineering progresses and leads to redrafting to correct the error and potential back charges. This can make the difference between a profit and a loss. Company E also understands that undetected design/engineering errors lead to costly field rework for the engineering company.

A thorough review of customer supplied documentation for errors upon receipt and an independent checking of drawings and documents before dispatch are therefore part of the process to eliminate errors.

Accordingly, Company E goes to great lengths to ensure that all its draftsmen understand that they must "Do it right first time."

The Empowerment Paradigm employee instinctively understands that eliminating errors will not only increase profitability, of which they partake, but enhances the company image with customers and may lead to further orders.

Choosing the Right Quality Management System

The simplification of function and documentation automatically conferred by the Empowerment Paradigm Difference, and as discussed earlier in this chapter, will be reflected in a clear and concise quality management system with quality procedures that are designed to support organizational functions rather than constrain, or change, them by dictate.

This ethos is reinforced by project managers who are accountable for the bottom line of their projects. Not only do project managers know that in-house work should be error-free, but they are also keenly cognizant that project suppliers should minimize nonconformities. In short, project managers understand that a low price without quality is ultimately not cost-effective. Accordingly, project managers select, and have sole responsibility for, which suppliers are used on their project. Project managers are therefore tied into the performance of the suppliers. The Empowerment Paradigm organization intuitively understands the value of supplier relationships and uses them extensively as a way to increase operational effectiveness, minimize nonconformities and expensive corrective actions, and so increase margins. Project managers therefore cultivate and build strong relationships with reliable suppliers, whose performance adds significant value to the execution of the project. This includes conferring sole supplier status in exchange for the highest levels of reliability and quality, introducing trial-fits in the supplier's works, implementing piece-marked deliveries to improve the goods received, storage, and the construction process. Suppliers so selected must have qualified for approved supplier status under the organization's quality management system and possess a proven track record of successful supply with the organization.

Case Study

Company E subcontracts the fabrication of steelwork, which is then supplied piecemeal to site for field erection of a modular design.

The subcontractor is required to fabricate the steelwork to exacting standards of quality with quality control measures as stipulated within an inspection and test plan.

The Empowerment Paradigm Difference dictates that Company E's project managers will consider the quality regime of this subcontractor to be an extension of their own quality management system and so spend time ensuring that both systems work congruously by intervention where necessary. This extends to becoming involved in the supplier's inspection and test plan, attending important inspections, such as the final, predispatch, trail fit of modular steelwork, and ensuring all quality documentations are properly prepared, signed, and certified.

Such attention to detail at the subcontractor's works substantially reduces on-site modifications, which cost up to ten times more in the field than in the shop.

Management Review and Participation

Senior management play a vital role in ensuring that an organization's quality management system is operating correctly and remains fit for purpose. This starts with the management review process, as stipulated within ISO 9000, but extends far beyond this in the Empowerment Paradigm organization.

Senior management within the Empowerment Paradigm organization will naturally understand the importance of their participation in the quality management system and will take rigorous steps to support the quality function.

In the first instance, they will ensure, by periodic review and oversight of quality audits, that the quality management system is not constraining operational efficiency by overprescriptive bureaucratic procedures. As stated earlier in this section, the quality management system should guide and assist the organization's operations, not impede them.

Secondly, they ensure that the organizational quality ethos is properly communicated and taken seriously by all employees. This starts by giving all employees a comprehensive quality induction, describing their specific responsibilities to quality and explaining the tangible rewards that flow from reduced error costs. The organizational quality message is reinforced at every opportunity. This is achieved in diverse ways, including in newsletters or general memorandums when particular examples of the importance of quality arise.

Finally, senior management should ensure the effectiveness of the quality management system empirically. In most organizations, this can be achieved by analyzing the number and cost of errors. Project managers, as part of their functional remit, are therefore expected to produce a cost-per-error report on a periodic basis. By comparison to previous periods, error trends can be easily identified, and corrective and preventative actions devised and implemented.

Accountable Leadership Reduces Errors

By incentivizing project managers in the Empowerment Paradigm organization and making them accountable for the bottom line of the project, quality is automatically improved at the functional hub of operations. Just as projects managers represent the organization in dealing with customers, they are also the face of the organization for suppliers. Project managers within the Empowerment Paradigm organization will instinctively understand the importance of supplier activities and will invest time in ensuring the quality of a supplier's goods/services.

Measuring the Effectiveness of the Quality Management System

The Empowerment Paradigm organization's multifunctional project managers and project team members help in the identification and resolution of errors at the source. They also evaluate nonconformities in order to spot trends and generic faults that can be remedied for future projects. Porous project boundaries with interchangeable project managers and team members ensure these trends and generic problems are properly communicated, and lessons learned on individual projects become the collective property of the organization. By involving all project team members in evaluating nonconformities and formulating resolutions, the cost of corrective actions, in terms of replicating a function and remedial measures, become common knowledge within the organization, ensuring effective corrective and preventative actions can be implemented and the error count and associated costs minimized. Since, in the Empowerment Paradigm organization, unnecessary costs impact upon the employees' reward, every team member is incentivized to eliminate nonconformities, and actively participate in the corrective and preventative process.

By respecting these principles, the Empowerment Paradigm organization knows it can rely upon an exemplary level of quality and can confidently market this virtue. Customers prefer organizations that don't make mistakes—it adds to their own value.

Quality Outcomes

Superb project execution, on-time deliveries, and exemplary quality of supply almost always result in preferred, or even sole, supplier status. This is the ultimate and most powerful accolade a customer can confer upon an organization and is the attainable goal and natural reward of all the Empowerment Paradigm organizations.

Health and Safety

Put Health and Safety First

Health and safety plays a vital role in employee welfare, organizational reputation, and commercial success. The Empowerment Paradigm Difference ensures that this is recognized at all levels of an organization and considerable time and effort is expended in attaining and maintaining the highest levels of health and safety outcomes.

Investing in Employee Welfare

The Empowerment Paradigm organization has a serious commitment to the welfare of its employees, enshrined within values and propagated by senior management and designed to sit congruously alongside a stringent and rigorously controlled health and safety regime. Senior management understands the importance of ensuring employee welfare. They constantly monitor and review health and safety systems, procedures, and statistics and ensure resources are made available to invest in measures to protect the health and safety of employees in the knowledge that not to do so is commercially counterproductive. Sick and injured employees are not productive. Safety incidents often lead to costly insurance and legal charges. Moreover, declining health and safety statistics are likely to result in an organization being blacklisted across an entire industry sector (or more than one).

Case Study

Company F supplies high-tech pollution control equipment installed at height on power station chimneys. Before embracing the Empowerment Paradigm philosophy, an employee of Company F had been seriously injured on site. Investigations identified out-of-date safety equipment as a contributory factor in the accident. Company F was blacklisted by several major customers, following the incident.

The Empowerment Paradigm Difference dictates to invest in new, state-of-the-art safety equipment to improve the morale and productivity of employees. It also enables Company F to re-establish its reputation with customers for safe working. Eventually, Company F is removed from all blacklists and substantially increases its booking.

In the Empowerment Paradigm organization, employees are secure in the knowledge that their welfare is paramount and that the organization will not put this at risk for commercial gain. Reciprocally, in contrast to other organizations, employees intuitively understand that the organization's commercial success, together with their own welfare and job security, is tightly bound to the observance by all of the strictures of an appropriately stringent health and safety regime. This is the automatic benefit derived from the Empowerment Paradigm Difference.

Employee Commitment to Health and Safety

This mutual respect and understanding allow employees, in the knowledge that senior management are fully committed to their safety and welfare, to operate within the framework of the health and safety regime free of fear with efforts channeled more effectively toward operational duties.

The Empowerment Paradigm organization's naturally enhanced levels of communication and cooperation, together with responsibility and accountability for functional performance devolved to the lowest levels, ensure that peer pressure plays an active role in compliance to health and safety requirements.

Accountability Mitigates Risk

As in many other aspects within the Empowerment Paradigm organization, empowered and accountable project managers play a key role in ensuring compliance to health and safety strictures. They understand the importance of health and safety in all project activities, paying particular attention to those occurring on site or on customer premises. This includes not only ensuring all safety procedures are followed without exception but ensuring that all project personnel, especially those located at a job site, are properly trained for their task, understand the safety aspects of their duties explicitly, and have at their disposal and use the best, properly certified safety equipment. Safety violations are anathema to these project managers who know that the cost impact of even a single violation has the potential to impact across the organization.

Statistical Analysis

In a similar vein to the monitoring of errors within the quality management system, senior management ensures the effectiveness of the health and safety regime empirically. In most organizations, this can be achieved by analyzing the number and cost of lost-time incidents and sick days taken. The Empowerment Paradigm organization also ensures that safety incidents are evaluated and compared to other similar incidents. Trends can be easily identified, and corrective and preventative actions devised and implemented. Monitoring sick days can also reveal an underlying problem with employee welfare that can also be identified and addressed.

Managing Incidents

In the Empowerment Paradigm organization, senior management are fully cognizant of the risks posed in respect of accident incident rates and take steps to ensure they, and all project managers, are properly trained to manage the impact of health and safety incidents.

Most customers recognize a national health and safety monitoring scheme based upon the number, seriousness, and insurance cost payout of recordable health and safety incidents. An incident rate, based upon such criteria, is established for all organizations working with or bidding for work with the customer.

Case Study

Company F is bidding for a high-profile, high-value phase 2 contract with a large power station operator. Company F is currently on-site, completing phase 1 work. Several long-standing subcontractors of the power station operator are bidding for the phase 2 work.

The power station operator has a target zero initiative with respect to safety-related incidents and monitors the experience modification rate (EMR) of its subcontractors as a measure of this. The EMR is an insurance industry statistical measure that assesses not only the number of lost-time safety incidents but the cost in terms of insurance payouts. Incident management is therefore vital in mitigating costs and keeping the EMR low. The power station operator excludes bids for site work from those subcontractors with an EMR of 1.0 and above.

The Empowerment Paradigm Difference dictates that Company F understands the need to manage safety incidents properly and to minimize consequential insurance payouts. Its EMR is, accordingly, less than 1.0, allowing it to bid for phase 2 work. Of the five other subcontractors also wanting to bid for phase 2 work, all but one is excluded because of an EMR above 1.0. By managing the safety incidents in the Empowerment Paradigm way, Company F is rewarded by entering a considerably less competitive bidding process.

It is now common practice for customers to set an incident rate, above which an organization is removed from the bidding list. Such is the sensitivity of the incident rate that a single relatively minor incident, if not managed correctly so as to minimize the impact in terms of lost-time days and insurance payouts, has the potential to take the incident rate above that set by customers as a prerequisite for bidding. This can have a catastrophic effect upon an organization, possibly wiping out a huge proportion of its forecast revenue at a single stroke.

In this vital respect, the Empowerment Paradigm Difference, with its automatic benefits in health and safety, may serve as the dividing line between commercial success and abject failure.

Environmental

Environmental Awareness

Through its clearly defined and thoroughly propagated vision, mission, and values, the Empowerment Paradigm organization, in contrast to other organizations, is keenly aware of its place within, and its impact upon, the environment. Built-in mechanisms ensure that the organization automatically adopts policies that limit its environmental impact. This is the Empowerment Paradigm Difference.

Proactively Limiting Environmental Impact

Senior management ensures that the impact of the organization's operations is fully assessed. Measures are taken to minimize such impact or to ensure that the impact is offset in an environmentally responsible way. Environmental policy must include, where appropriate, plans to deal with environmental emergencies related to the organization's operations.

In today's business environment, having a visible environmental profile is essential. It is an ISO 14000 requirement; customers expect it and may even insist upon it. The Empowerment Paradigm organization instinctively understands that it must do more than pay lip service to the environment; it must make a meaningful, and visible, commitment to mitigating its operational environmental impact and make a contribution to general environmental causes.

Many of the organizational improvements discussed in this chapter automatically reduce an organization's environmental impact.

Case Study

Company G is looking at ways of reducing costs and its impact upon the environment.

The Empowerment Paradigm Difference ensures that Company G innovates to reduce costs in ways that are congruous with its environmental profile. It therefore introduces energy-saving measures such as improved insulation of buildings, the exclusive use of low-energy light bulbs, and ensuring heating and cooling systems are properly serviced and turned down when offices are closed.

In addition to this, Company G introduces and strictly adheres to a recycling program, including properly separating waste for disposal—paper, electrical goods, batteries, etc.

Built-in Environmental Cognizance

The Empowerment Paradigm organization is constantly striving to improve its products/services, and one aspect in the improvement process is limiting the environmental impact by the selection of environmentally friendly materials and performance that meet or exceed regulatory environmental requirements.

Once again, in the Empowerment Paradigm organization, empowered and accountable project managers understand the importance of minimizing the environmental impact of project activities and will be properly trained to understand potential environmental hazards and how to deal with any incidents that arise. In particular, project managers will ensure that they are familiar with local environmental regulations and that project procedures and practices reflect these. This will include matters such as responsible disposal of waste products so as not to pollute the local environment.

Maintaining Local Reputation

Good relations with the local community are well worth cultivating. In the first instance, it is entirely possible that many employees are part of that community. Through the philanthropic endeavors of its employees, the Empowerment Paradigm organization interacts with the local community. In this way, the organization is able to understand how its activities impact upon that community and the local environment and how this can be mitigated.

Case Study

Company G has a fabrication shop that is working on shifts and causing unacceptable noise pollution to local residents.

The Empowerment Paradigm Difference dictates that Company G should consider altering its shift pattern to lessen the impact or provide improved noise attenuation measures to those closest to the works.

Company G is planning to extend its works and understands that building goodwill with local residents may be of benefit when local planning consent is sought.

Intuitively understanding organizational responsibility to the general, and local, environment and its importance to the repute and operational success are the natural benefits derived from the Empowerment Paradigm Difference.

Sales and Proposals

Naturally Incentivized

An efficient and effective sales and proposals function is vital to an organization's commercial success. In contrast to other organizations, in the Empowerment Paradigm organization, the sales-and-proposals function is naturally incentivized, cost-efficient, self-correcting, and supported by and integrated with other parts of the organization. This is the Empowerment Paradigm Difference.

The Role of the Sales Manager

The sales-and-proposals function is served by sales teams led by a sales manager. The sales manager's role corresponds to that of the project manager. As such, sales managers are fully responsible and accountable for their remit. In the Empowerment Paradigm organization, sales managers and their team members intuitively understand that sales costs must be controlled, proposals to success rates analyzed, and high-margin projects should be pursued. In short, the contract award is not deemed a success unless that sale leads to a profit.

The Sales Team

The relationship between sales and project teams is therefore fundamental to the Empowerment Paradigm methodology. Sales teams are the conduits between the organization and the market. It is through the information provided by sales teams that the organization understands the size and structure of the available market for its selected product/service portfolio. Sales managers therefore ensure that the sales team comprises team members that between them have a full knowledge of the product/service they are selling and the market place, understand customer and regulatory requirements, and can provide information regarding new products/services that competitors are marketing and that may require a response.

The Empowerment Paradigm Difference ensures that sales team members are incentivized to not only look at what the market needs but also at competitor activity and pass on this information. Sales team members must duly understand Client's requirements, be aware of Companies performance on recent projects executed for that Client and try to obtain preferred vendor status well before the competition becomes aware of the project. This attitude of sales team members enables Company to maintain or increase its market share and book projects at acceptable margins.

Case Study

Company H designs and supplies air-conditioning systems for large commercial buildings. Impending environmental legislation in Company H's largest sales market requires a change in coolant gas for new installations and an upgrade of existing systems by 2014. Company H's major competitor is offering a discount on upgrades to organizations who place new installations with them.

The Empowerment Paradigm Difference ensures that sales team members are incentivized to look at competitor activity and pass on this information. Accordingly, Company H becomes aware of the competitor's offer, and a sales manager alerts senior management. Company H formulates a response that enables it to compete and retain its market share while protecting margins.

Conversely, project teams provide sales teams with experience and knowledge gained during the execution of a project. In the Empowerment Paradigm organization, porous team boundaries and good intraorganizational communication propagate the flow of knowledge and act as drivers for product/service improvements and innovative developments that can lead to new products/services and technologies.

Building and Maintaining Customer Relations

All sales team members are representatives of their organization, and just as a project manager *is* the organization after the award of contract, a sales representative *is* the organization prior to the award of contract. The Empowerment Paradigm organization intuitively understands the fundamental importance of this role and ensures that sales managers understands and communicate to customers the organization's carefully constructed vision, mission, and values.

The value of good customer relations during project execution is a vital sales tool that can lead to repeat orders and even preferred/sole supplier status. As such, the Empowerment Paradigm organization sales managers and project managers liaise regularly with respect to any problems that arise during project execution, the latter imparting information that may lead to a sale.

The decision to pursue an enquiry, or to decline, is critical to an organization's commercial success. In the Empowerment Paradigm organization, experienced sales managers, accountable for the bottom line, are incentivized to assess the seriousness of an enquiry, its likely success, and its profitability at an early stage. Such sales managers will decline to bid where the bid margin is likely to be too low or the prospects of a sale are not good or worth the effort.

Controlling the Costs of the Sales and Proposals Function

Major cost centers of the sales and proposals function are man-hours and business travel. In the Empowerment Paradigm organization, these costs are automatically monitored by empowered and accountable sales managers.

However, it is easy for a salesman or, indeed, a sales team to run up massive expenses in what might seem the reasonable pursuit of a contract. It is therefore absolutely necessary to ensure that the prospects of a sale are properly assessed prior to incurring substantial man-hours, travel, or other costs.

Just as a project manager may ask whether it is necessary for more than one project team member to travel to site, a sales manager should ask a similar question with regard to the size of the sales team that needs to visit a prospective customer. Good sales managers will travel by themselves when a large, profitable contract is in the offering rather than send a less-experienced salesperson.

Case Study

Company H's sales team ran up several tens of thousands of dollars in travel and hotel expenses in pursuit of a contract in the Caribbean. Although a reasonably sized contract with a major customer, the competition was fierce and the margins low. The prospects for a sale at a standard margin were low. So even in the event of the contract being awarded, all the contingency budget and much of the margin had been eroded by the sales team's expenses.

The Empowerment Paradigm Difference automatically ensures that the prospect for a sale, together with anticipated margins, are properly assessed prior to incurring high levels of expenditure in pursuit of the contract.

As with project managers and execution of projects, the Empowerment Paradigm sales manager is not only responsible for the sales function but is also accountable for the cost incurred. Accordingly, all sales team members know and trust that savings that are made in pursuit of a sale are both recognized and rewarded. In this way, sales team members afford the organization the room to offer larger rewards to its employees and so are directly determining, and contributing to, the level of their remuneration and bonus.

Meeting Market Demand at the Right Price

In the Empowerment Paradigm, the sales manager ensures that inquiries are properly received and that the proposals effort is productively focused in order to meet customer specifications and general requirements. The sales manager will be aware of prevalent, competitive pricing levels in the market for the organization's product/service and, in conjunction with an assigned project manager, will ensure proper margins and contingencies are priced in. Input from the contract and commercial functions also inform the price bid, avoiding unnecessarily harsh contract conditions and cash flow issues for project execution.

Qualitative Improvements

Qualitative Improvements

Qualitative improvements realized in Empowerment Paradigm organizations relate to the more intangible ways in which an organization has been enhanced, specifically, its effectiveness and efficiency and its professional and social cohesiveness. Two particular aspects are considered in detail, namely as follows:

OPTIMIZATION

Understanding how best to excel

TEAM BUILDING

Supporting each other and the community with genuine understanding and compassion

Optimization

The Futility of Maximization

Organizations employing the Empowerment Paradigm methodology will intuitively understand the vital difference between maximization and optimization.

Maximization is a blind, and crudely wasteful, objective. Maximization creates empires and bureaucratic monstrosities, which feed upon themselves and diminish the bottom line.

The Empowerment Paradigm Difference results in organizations that are automatically tuned to optimize rather than maximize. Every action undertaken by such organizations is defined by its objective of empowering the individual employee to create, innovate, and improve profitability.

The Empowerment Paradigm organization understands that it cannot grow too quickly, take on too large contract values, or service too diversified a product/technology portfolio. Increased margins are incentivized, not increased turnover, and margins can only being increased once a product/technology is fully understood and so, completely within the control of the organization.

Case Study

Engineering Company I provides installations to the power generation sector. This company designs, supplies, installs, and commissions its supply. Typically, 60 percent of a contract value relates to installation. However, installation is notoriously problematic and subject to factors outside of Company I's control (for example, weather and unions) and often leads to difficulties in terms of cash flow and low, or negative, margins.

The Empowerment Paradigm Difference ensures that Company I will, by its very nature, withdraw from the installation market and protect its cash flow and margin.

In the Empowerment Paradigm organization, an unchecked and isolated drive toward maximization is never an option. The organization recognizes its own capabilities and limits. It will never take on work in an area outside of its field of knowledge and expertise. In this way, it avoids unacceptable and unmanageable risk. Customers invariably welcome the honesty of being told by a supplier that they cannot bid for a contract because it is outside an organization's capability or comfort zone.

Case Study

Engineering Company I has an annual turnover of $80 million. It is invited by a customer who has been impressed by previous performance to bid for a contract worth $200 million.

The Empowerment Paradigm Difference ensures that Company I automatically recognizes that a contract of this size, together with work already in progress, will put unreasonable strains upon its engineering resources and finances. It admits as such to the customer who, appreciates the honesty, divides the scope, and gives Company I a smaller and manageable contract for $45 million—still the largest single contract in its history.

Sustainable Diversity of Output

The Empowerment Paradigm organization also understands that it cannot grow its product/service portfolio too quickly. New products and technologies must be thoroughly understood by the organization and tested on a trial basis prior to full market offering.

The Empowerment Paradigm Difference dictates that when the Company is not fully familiar with a new technology it cannot accept the risk of that technology not working as designed on multiple projects. Only after the new technology works on the first project and after that project passed the performance test the Company is in a position to accept additional projects at a significant lower risk. To accept multiple projects with unproven technology can lead to severe commercial and reputational damage.

Case Study

Engineering Company I acquires a new technology that is keenly sought after by its customers.

The Empowerment Paradigm Difference ensures that Company I instinctively recognizes that it is not fully familiar with the technology and understands the risk of the technology not working as designed in the field. Accordingly, Company I takes on only one project for the new, unproven technology.

Once the technology is working and meeting design specifications, Company I is in a position to take on more projects at a significantly reduced risk.

The company intent on maximization would take as many contracts as possible for the new, unproven technology and risk severe commercial and reputational damage should it not work first time or subsequently fail.

Project Management Attuned to Optimization

Project managers, intent upon optimization, will put pressure on senior management to take all necessary measures to protect and enhance the bottom line. Likewise, project team members are empowered and encouraged to apply the same pressure to the project managers. This further illustrates the benefits of the bottom-up, self-determining approach embodied by the Empowerment Paradigm Difference.

Team Building

The Transformative Effects

The most obvious improvement derived from introducing the Empowerment Paradigm methodology to an organization is the transformative effect of team building.

This manifests itself throughout the Empowerment Paradigm organization as a natural consequence of the introduction of the measures described in the first four chapters.

It starts with employees identifying with a well-conceived and aspirational organizational identity as set out in the vision, mission, and values. This sense of collective purpose encourages employees to understand that individual success is rooted in cooperation and to reach out to each other to this end.

The removal of fear engenders within individuals the confidence to communicate with fellow employees, at all levels, to express new ideas, and to become involved with implementing the ideas of others. Even the most insular and reticent employees invariably become involved eventually.

Open lines of communication, vertically and horizontally, uncover problems that might otherwise remain hidden, and affords employees, at all levels, the opportunity to support colleagues and assist in resolving the problems.

Encouraging employees to attain multifunctionality increases the understanding of the roles of others within the organization and enables employees to support one another in those roles.

Refocusing organizational orientation to become project-centered creates multidisciplinary project teams with porous boundaries and interchangeable project managers and project team members and removes the barriers inherent within departmental orientated organizations.

The ability of employees, through their own actions, to determine the level of their remuneration and bonuses encourages them to ensure that fellow employees do not fail and are supported professionally in every possible respect.

Employees understand that they will benefit most by directing their individual competitiveness to the collective success of the organization and that subversive politicking undermines this process. In the Empowerment Paradigm organization, this will be swiftly eliminated by peer pressure, backed by management.

All of these factors, explored previously, ensure that the ultimate product of the Empowerment Paradigm Difference is a tight-knit and cohesive corporate team incentivized toward a common goal.

Organizational Inclusiveness

Social activities promote employee bonding and allow employees an insight into their colleagues' personal lives, which enhances understanding and empathy and allows employees the confidence and freedom to intervene when colleagues need support and assistance in their personal lives. In the Empowerment Paradigm organization, employees will intuitively know that they can ask for this support and assistance without fear of being perceived as weak. In the Empowerment Paradigm organization, employees will also know that it is OK to offer such support without offense or undue intrusion.

Employees' partners and relatives are welcomed into the ambit of the organization so as to engender an understanding of the demands the organization's places upon the employees and so helps reduce the inevitable tension between work and personal life.

Enhanced transparency allows employees to feel an integral part of the organization's plans.

Case Study

A shop floor worker at Company J loses his wife and all his possessions in a house fire. It transpires that he has no insurance.

Company J espouses the principles of team building encouraged and automatically derived from the Empowerment Paradigm Difference.

Employees at Company J immediately, and without prompting, offer comfort and support to the bereaved worker and hold a collection, which raises thousands of dollars. The management of Company J is aware of this and doubles the collected amount.

The Empowerment Paradigm Difference ensures that all employees know that they can rely on this kind of support from both colleagues and management.

The Empowerment Paradigm employees understand that they are valued by the organization. This leads to an increased sense of self-worth and well-being, which in turn affords employees the confidence to reach out to colleagues.

Mutual Compassion and Support

The Empowerment Paradigm organization intuitively understands the value of its team spirit and allows it to shrive and grow. The ultimate manifestation of this team spirit arrives when employees approach management of their own volition and ask permission to contribute to the local community and causes. This is a sign of an organization that is collectively mature, confident, and selfless enough to consider those in need. This is the Empowerment Paradigm Difference. Believe in its virtues and implement its methodology faithfully, and the transformative effect of team building is remarkably rewarding.

Chapter Six

Recognizing the Complete
Empowerment Paradigm Organization

The Complete Empowerment Paradigm Organization

If the measures described within chapters 2, 3, and 4 are faithfully instituted within an organization, unremittingly reiterated, and robustly supported by senior management, the organizational improvements described in the preceding chapter will automatically ensue. The resulting organization can be described as the Complete Empowerment Paradigm organization. Such an organization is distinct in that, once a direction has been set by senior management, the day-to-day operations are determined by the actions of the empowered employees at all levels of the organization.

But how does one know when such an objective has been achieved? The Complete Empowerment Paradigm organization has various attributes, which clearly identify it. Such attributes include the following:

Inspired and Trusted Leadership

The CEO will be completely trusted by employees, demonstrate honesty and integrity, show compassion and understanding towards employees and their families, promote a positive goal-orientated outlook for organizational prospects, create a rounded team of talented managers, lead by example and show unwavering support of the organization's vision, mission, and values.

Fear-Free Atmosphere

Employees will be more content, and it shows. The difference between employees who are working in an atmosphere where fear lurks at every turn to that which pervades the Empowerment Paradigm organization is immense. Employees smile, are open and cordial with each other, and generally perform their work with an ease and openness that is missing when employees are in constant fear. In this environment, no one fears failure or fears what management or colleagues will think of decisions that are made. Mistakes are freely admitted, immediately communicated, and met with a "how can I help" attitude. The uncertainty and distraction of job security are substantially diminished because all employees are informed about the direction and financial state of the organization and understand the future prospects. Every idea for improvement or a reduction in cost is welcomed, and employees need not fear that their ideas will be ridiculed, nor will they scheme against or seek to undermine each other, knowing that to do so will impact upon collective success as so individual reward.

It is impossible to overemphasize the transformation within the general atmosphere of a fear-free organization. Just by walking into the office, it is immediately obvious that a more positive, friendlier, more productive working environment prevails. This is the most obvious sign that the Empowerment Paradigm methodology is working.

Enhanced Sense of Direction and Purpose

Equally apparent within the Complete Empowerment Paradigm organization is an enhanced sense of individual and collective purpose.

With a clearly defined and enthusiastically propagated organizational vision and mission, supported by a set of guiding and inspirational values, employees understand their sense of direction and functional role and are imbued with a sense of worth and purpose that are absent from other organizations.

In the Complete Empowerment Paradigm organization, employees are rarely unsure of what to do and to what end they are working. If this does occur, colleagues will intervene to correct and redirect. In this way, idleness is minimized, and resources are assigned to meaningful and productive areas.

Improved Interaction

A further sign that the Complete Empowerment Paradigm organization has been attained relates to the way in which employees interact with each other and with senior management.

Firstly, by communicating openly with each other, management will discover that employees are able to resolve many of the problems that arise themselves. If needed, employees will ask for help with, or freely admit to, their own difficulties and mistakes and volunteer to help others with their own.

Management will also discover that they naturally become more informed about what is happening throughout the organization because employees openly communicate with them. Problems are shared and not hidden.

Increased Innovation

Managers of the Complete Empowerment Paradigm organization will be amazed at the willingness of employees at all levels of skill and competence to strive to innovate. Employees will no longer feel constrained in expressing ideas to improve their function and that of others. Indeed, managers encourage and reward those putting forward these ideas.

In this way, existing products are improved by employees who are eager to ensure these are the best available on the market and will go to extraordinary lengths to serve the sales-and-proposals function by offering these improvements to the marketplace.

Such close interaction with the sales-and-proposals function also enables product designers and innovators to understand market demands, ensuring niche or new markets, for improved or new products/technologies are identified and served.

Improved Productivity

The Complete Empowerment Paradigm organization will reveal itself by its significantly improved productivity.

Confident, aspirational, multifunctional employees will naturally extend their functional remit. Empowered and accountable project and sales managers ensure that project man-hours and other costs are monitored, controlled, and minimized. Contented employees will always work more productively. Project-focused operations and simplification of function drive down costs.

Ideas and innovations with respect to working methodology are freely exchanged through porous project and sales team boundaries, ensuring efficiencies are translated into improved productivity without distortion or delay.

Vastly Improved Quality

A key sign that the Complete Empowerment Paradigm organization has been attained is a marked improvement in the quality of output.

Driven by employees who understand that to innovate and reduce costs is to improve their chances of financial reward and reinforced by empowered and accountable project managers, the Complete Empowerment Paradigm organization constantly strives to satisfy its customers by getting it right on the first attempt.

Minimizing nonconformities extends to the activities of suppliers. The Complete Empowerment Paradigm organization understands that the quality of suppliers' goods/services is essential to this and so seeks to establish strong relationships with its suppliers in order to enhance the quality of its own supply and eliminate nonconformities within the organization's activities.

Empathy and Philanthropy

The Complete Empowerment Paradigm organization will exude individual and collective compassion.

Employees who encounter personal difficulties and bereavements are supported, emotionally and financially, at all levels of the organization. Employees understand that they are able to disclose their problems to colleagues and management without embarrassment or fear of consequences if these affect their performance at work. In this way, the Complete Empowerment Paradigm organization behaves like an extension to the family.

A significant indication that the Complete Empowerment Paradigm organization has been attained is the automatic desire of employees to want to help those less fortunate than themselves and to reach out to the local community. Philanthropy, in terms of financial support and time given to the community, flows from the contentedness of the workforce that, free of the constraints of self-preservation inherent in other organizations, is able to turn its attention to the plight of others.

Self-Perpetuating and Self-Determining Outcomes

Perhaps the most incredible aspect of the Complete Empowerment Paradigm organization is how little input is required by senior management once it has been achieved.

This, in and of itself, is a sign that the Empowerment Paradigm principles have been successfully instituted.

Understanding the principles set out in the first four chapters and faithfully implementing the recommendations contained therein determine the course for the organization. Thereafter, a surprisingly light hand on the tiller is all that is required to maintain that course.

Employees are incentivized to resolve their own difficulties by consulting colleagues, improve their skills to become multifunctional and thereby expand their function remit, create and innovate, simplify organizational function, focus attention and resources upon the profit generating function, improve quality, and reduce costs. Optimization of the organization and management of risk are automatically achieved by employees striving to attain these goals.

Senior management that can recognize this, and all the other attributes described above, will have attained the ultimate objective of the Empowerment Paradigm and, providing that hand on the tiller remains true in whatever waters are encountered, will long reap the rewards of commercial success with a contended, committed, and grateful workforce.